2 book

The Brain Challenge

Stop overthinking and boost your self-confidence. The practical training to unfu*k your mind, overcome indecision, stress, negative thoughts, and be more confident.

written by Sebastian O'Brien

Copyright © 2020 Sebastian O'Brien All rights reserved

No part of this book may be reproduced, or stored in a retrieval system, or transmitted in any form or by any means, electronic, mechanical, photocopying, recording, or otherwise, without express written permission of the publisher.

Cover design by: Sebastian O'Brien

To whom is trying to find a way to take the driver seat of their life:

Good luck.

Book 1

Self-confidence Training

A practical guide on how to face your fears and build unshakable self-esteem. Step outside your comfort zone, reach your goals and finally master your life! For men and women

written by Sebastian O'Brien

table of contents

Introduction — 01

Chapter 1 — 07
No one can make you feel inferior without your consent

Chapter 2 — 26
Setting goals is your road to the life you want

Chapter 3 — 51
You can, you should, and if you're brave enough to start, you will

Chapter 4 — 73
Facing your fears gives you strength, courage and confidence

Chapter 5 — 92
Take action and get to know yourself better

Chapter 6 — 116
You've got to experience failure to understand that you can survive it

Chapter 7 — 140
Believe you can and you're already halfway there

Conclusions — 161

Introduction

Congratulations! The fact that you picked up this book shows that you are already well aware that self-confidence is crucial in almost every aspect of life. It completely transforms both how we see ourselves, and how we are perceived by others - which means everything when it comes to our successes in life; whether in a professional or a personal context. To appear competent or worth someone's time, we must first believe our own hype. After all, if we are not even sure of ourselves, how on earth can we hope to convince others of our value?

You may feel shy, anxious, or simply fearful to change your current daily reality. You want to make something of yourself, but worry that you will fall flat on your face. You may ask yourself if it is really worth it to even try.

If you are unsuccessful this time, won't you be ashamed forever? Will other people remember you for it?

The answer to these questions, quite simply, is *no.* You cannot and should not go through life dwelling on every setback. If you fail, it means you took a risk and tried something. And whatever the outcome, this is something to be proud of, and to never stop doing.

And no, harsh as it may sound, nobody will remember every detail of what you did in your life - what went well and what didn't. As humans, we have a tendency to simplify things and look for the bigger picture. We cannot remember every detail about someone anyway, so we instinctively develop summaries about the people we know. And these summaries are what come to mind whenever we think about them.

So don't waste your energy worrying about the small stuff! You should aim to present the best version of yourself, sure, but fretting over every minor setback, or what you view as your weaknesses, will not help you to do this. Obsessing over your insecurities only draws attention to them but true self-confidence will outshine them. So if you focus on your strengths and find ways to thrive despite - or even because of - these "flaws," then the bigger picture others see will be an impressive one indeed.

Besides, we all spend *far* too much time and energy fretting over what others think about our every move. In truth, we are all more concerned about our own journey. Are you really lying awake at night thinking about how your acquaintance, Sally, tried to set up that catering business last year and it failed? Of course not - you're too focused on your own ambitions and challenges. And so, dear reader, is Sally.

If we all came to terms with the fact that most people really aren't thinking all that much about us - at least not in the way that we fear - then we would all feel a whole lot braver to think big and aim high.

Let me briefly introduce myself before we go any further. My name is Sebastian O'Brien and I was born in Ireland, 1969. I am a Psychotherapist and counselor with many years of experience working to support a whole range of individuals who are ready to finally live life in the driver's seat. I like to work in partnership with my clients to create an environment of good energy and trust. Working with individuals struggling with their self-confidence, to make a real difference in their lives, is what I truly love to do. And this is why I have written the self-confidence training you see before you.

The purpose of this book is to encourage you to believe in yourself. To not give up on your aspirations. To have the success you crave and deserve, and ultimately - to be happy. I will give you all the tools, perspective, and motivation you need to unlock the potential that's already within you, bursting to get out. And all of this is contained within one small but mighty term: *self-confidence.*

There's a common saying that it's not what we do that we will regret most, but what we *don't* do. Do you really want to live with regrets that you didn't follow your dreams, simply due to fear of how other people - who are mostly as anxious and uncertain as you are, believe me - would react if you failed once or twice?

You already have the raw materials to make your life truly marvellous - you just have to make the choice to use them. Alternatively, you can simply live passively, and just "get by," letting life happen to you without taking any real control over it. But life is beautiful. It is the greatest present you have ever and will ever receive. This is why you must take action: grab the pen and write your life as you have always dreamed it to be.

If you haven't reached your goals yet, you may simply need this little push in the right direction to get the ball rolling. You need to focus on yourself; to start a journey of self-discovery for a deeper understanding of what you can improve and change about how you view yourself, how you interact with others - and all the day-to-day challenges that you will face throughout your life.

We are all wonderfully different individuals - but in the way that counts, we all are the same. And so, we all react the same way to the right input. This book will provide you with that input. I will help you to find balance between self-confidence and humility. Between striving for the best and accepting your setbacks. Between pushing your limits and being forgiving and kind to yourself.

I believe that by developing awareness and moving beyond temporary "quick fixes" and instead implementing long-lasting changes - you can better develop the skills and attitudes that will help you lead a more gratifying life.

Let me give you an example I like to use with many clients who struggle with self-belief. Do you know who Edison was - yes, Thomas Edison? Well, when he was still in school, his teacher said that he was "too stupid" to be able to learn anything. As you may have heard, in 1878, he went on to invent the long-lasting commercially viable incandescent lightbulb. Edison's original "lightbulb moment" had a *huge* impact on society. He quite literally lit up the world, and held 1,093 patents to his name by the time of his death. But do you think it was easy for him? Not at all. He failed thousands of times trying to make his dream a reality. But for both his and for all our sakes - thank goodness he didn't give up so easily.

I could offer you hundreds of examples like this one - but that's beside the point. The point is that y*ou* are the only one who can control your own life. You can reach anything - despite what others may have led you to believe during your life. Of course, in this world nothing is plain sailing, but with great dedication and hard work, you can do it - whatever "it" may be for you.

I am not, I regret to inform you, selling a ticket to paradise or offering you everything you desire on a plate. However, if you overcome the self-doubt you're currently grappling with - and you put in all the necessary effort, you will be able to reach it for yourself. This is my promise.

Ultimately, I will show you how to tap into a new realm of self-confidence to transform your passive life into an active one.

To help you in this you will find self-analysis exercises at the end of each chapter. They may seem easy at first glance, but they are really important to get the most out of this book as possible. They are not the types of exercises where you walk away with a grade or score- but simply with a better understanding of the workings of your own mind. Before improving your self-confidence, you must get to deeply know yourself.. If you take them seriously, they are a powerful tool for self-analysis and becoming a better person.

Live every single moment at your full capacity, and you won't have any regrets. Self-confidence is the key to success.

Chapter 1

No one can make you feel inferior without your consent

Let's get started with some definitions. Self-confidence, self-esteem, self-efficacy, and self-acceptance... aren't they all essentially the same thing?

You will, no doubt, have an overall picture of what we're talking about when we mention these terms. But I find that a basic understanding of the subtle differences - the specific areas of self-worth which they cover - is a great way to recognize which areas you struggle with personally. Most likely, you are stronger in some areas than others, but are not sure which. This can make it unclear how to pinpoint your areas for improvement.

Well, let's break it down:

Self-Confidence

You may feel like this one is a no-brainer, but researchers actually have a tough time recognizing on what, exactly, self-confidence is. Some say it's merely "believing in yourself," while others go into more detail about the expectations you have for your life and capabilities, and your subconscious self-evaluation. For non-academic purposes, however, to be self-confident is essentially to trust in our own abilities and believe that we can do whatever we set our minds to.

Along with shaping the beliefs you hold about yourself, self-confidence is a trait that permeates your thoughts, feelings, and actions. Think about a confident person you know. Okay - now have a think about *how* you know this person is confident. You can't know for sure what someone is thinking or feeling, so you base your judgment of their self-confidence on their words, actions, or overall demeanor. You should have at least some degree of self-belief to have self-confidence, but of course - this isn't the whole story.

Why Self-Confidence is so Important

The more confident you become, the more you will be able to quieten the voice inside you that says, "*I can't,*" replacing it with louder and more positive affirmations, being able to reassure yourself of your worth and capacities, completely independently of any external praise or validation. In other words, compliments from others are great, and all, but our self-worth can't depend on this kind of feedback. We must discover for ourselves how to be completely self-reliant when it comes to self-confidence in order to strengthen it. Otherwise, although you may feel unstoppable after some positive feedback, on the reverse side of the coin, the slightest negative reaction can completely floor you.

As social creatures, we tend to feel good when approved and validated by those around us. And although this is not essentially unhealthy, ranking our entire value according to the opinions of others is a surefire way to never feel truly satisfied or self-confident. We will constantly seek praise as an external confirmation that we are good enough. This is a trap we all fall into, at least occasionally. But why do we value the opinions of others so much more than our own in this way? Why isn't our own approval enough?

Because we lack self-confidence!

And of course - the social media revolution has only intensified this obsession with how we're perceived, as we base our self-worth upon the superficial representations of ourselves online. This may be your Facebook profile picture, your satirical tweet, or your LinkedIn bio - the craving for approval is the common thread. No, we don't have to unsubscribe from this often-vital modern may of communicating altogether, but we must reevaluate our approach to how we value ourselves. If you feel deeply better about yourself when a photo you upload or a funny comment you share gets a lot of likes -

this can become harmful. You become slowly addicted to the little highs you get with every dopamine-boosting notification, so much so that when they don't come in as you hope, you may feel that your self-worth has also run short.

Self-confidence Through Learning and Growing

Building true self-confidence means taking small steps that leave a lasting sense of accomplishment within yourself. If you've ever learned a language, reached a fitness goal, mastered a skill, or overcome any setback to get to where you wanted to be, you will know what I'm talking about. Because you do these things for yourself - and not merely to get the attention or thumbs-up (whether physically, metaphorically or indeed, digitally!) from your peers.

If you think back to any of your key accomplishments in life, you'll likely find that it took a lot of perseverance. If you could triumph through adversity then, it's only logical for me to suggest that you can do it again (and again) in other areas of your life.

As your self-confidence grows, you'll find yourself more driven to grow with it by pushing your limits and expanding your ambitions, setting your fears of failure to one side to make room for your hope for success. On top of all that, self-confidence provides you with the skills and coping mechanisms to handle failure. Self-confidence doesn't mean you won't sometimes face failures. However, thanks to the inner-strength you will cultivate, you will be able to choose to learn and grow from your setbacks instead of feeling crippled by them, and letting them define your self-worth, or take away your baseline of self-esteem.

Trust me - as you keep pushing yourself to try new things, you'll start to truly understand how failure and mistakes lead to personal growth. You will reach content and comforting acceptance that failure is simply a part of life: it doesn't suggest anything negative about you, but merely proves that you are pushing yourself. Paradoxically, by being more ready to fail, you'll actually succeed more — this because you're not expecting for everything to be 100 percent perfect before you act. You become less fearful to take the plunge. And it's a question of probability that the more ventures you attempt, the more successful ones you will one day have under your belt.

Self-confident – but not self-absorbed!

Now it might seem counterintuitive to say this, but when you have more self-confidence, you actually become less focused on yourself. Let me explain. We've all been guilty of stepping into a room and thinking, *"they are all looking at me"* or *"they are all judging me."* The truth is that, people are wrapped up in their own thoughts and concerns. When you get out of your own head, you'll be able to genuinely engage with others, focusing more on what they actually have to say, rather than what you fear they are thinking about *you*.

You'll enjoy your interactions more because you won't be so concerned about what kind of impression you're making, and you won't be comparing yourself to others. Your relaxed state will most likely put others at ease as well, helping you to establish deeper connections and come across as a much more self-assured, competent person.

Self-confidence can also breed deeper empathy for those around you. This is because when you're fully present as a result of freeing yourself from this self-conscious internal angst, you're more likely to notice the needs and subtle cues of others. When you're not preoccupied with your own self-doubt, you can be there for other people who may have their own internal struggles.

Finally, self-confidence roots you in who you really are - your "authentic self," if you will. By becoming more self-assured, you'll be able to accept your alleged weaknesses and personality quirks, knowing that they don't change your self-worth. This level of self-acceptance (more on this at the end of the chapter) is a groundbreaking step not only for your self-confidence, but also your overall self-esteem.

Self-Efficacy, Self-Esteem, and Self-Acceptance: What are they?

What about Self-Esteem?

Self-esteem is a more long-term way in which we value and perceive ourselves. It lies deeper within us than self-confidence, which can change on the hour and can be influenced by factors as trivial as how our hair is looking that day to the weather outside. This isn't to brush off self-confidence itself as trivial, of course. However, we must acknowledge its relative fluidity and openness to adapt to our transitory emotions.

Although self-esteem is also changeable, when compared to self-confidence, it is a relatively stable belief about one's overall self-worth. As such, it is more difficult than self-confidence to develop. But over time, if we build up our self-confidence, on a deeper level, our self-esteem will also be positively impacted. And due to this slow-moving and more solid nature, once built up, it is also much more resistant to what your life may throw at it. It can eventually become a grounding rock that you can rely on when times get tough, and your self-confidence fluctuates.

Our self-esteem begins to form in childhood, but can only expand to the degree that we feel valued by our parents. This is mainly due to the fact that before the age of eight, we lack the ability to formulate a clear sense of self—independent, that is, from the affirmations we receive from our guardians.

And so, if your parents didn't communicate the message that you are worthy and accepted—separate from our inevitable imperfect behaviors—you are likely conditioned to view yourself as inadequate, even today. If any parental praise depended exclusively on your actions, unfortunately, you will have the internalized belief that you are somehow *not enough*. As an unfortunate consequence, your self-esteem may be tarnished right up into adulthood.

But don't lose hope - as mentioned earlier - although building self-esteem is a long-game - it is still very much possible! And the long-term rewards are more than worth the effort.

Mainstream psychology teaches that self-esteem is made up of two distinct components: Our-self confidence, and how well we actually perform or realize our ambitions (self-efficacy). When these two boxes are ticked, and self-esteem is thus sufficiently lifted, we take the long and winding road to self-acceptance - our final glorious destination.

What on earth is Self-Efficacy?

Self-confidence is all well and good - but as just mentioned, unless you throw a healthy serving of self-efficacy into the mix - you're still going nowhere. That's because self-efficacy equates to putting yourself out there. You may learn to build up your self-confidence like a pro, but what are you going to do with all that freshly grown ego? You also have to take action to really grab life with both hands and put that self-confidence to good use.

Self-efficacy differs from self-confidence in an important way: the definition of self-confidence revolves around the ideas about your worth, while self-efficacy is rooted in your beliefs about your capabilities. In this sense, self-confidence is focused on essence and the present, while self-efficacy is based on actions and the future. And it's not much use having self-confidence if this has an expiry date, or if you aren't acting on it.

I often see clients finally make a breakthrough when it comes to how they look at themselves in the mirror every morning - they finally find the voice to speak up and the grit to seize each day. But what next? This kind of self-belief is only half-baked as this key component of self-efficacy is missing. Are you one of those people who thinks *"yeah, I guess I'm pretty competent. I can handle myself, and I acknowledge my strengths,"* only to still feel unfulfilled? To break into a cold sweat if someone asks where you plan to be in ten years time?

None of us can plan our whole lives out to every detail, and I am not implying that we should. But sticking your head in the sand at the thought of where your path is leading is only going to leave you feeling lost at some point down the line. So many of us are in denial when we think about our true desires. Are you really satisfied with your job - or are you just tired of pushing yourself for more and see staying put as the more appealing option right now? Are you truly happy drifting from one casual relationship to the next, or do you simply feel that this is better than the alternative of spending some time alone to work on yourself, or committing to someone in particular? But this isn't just about those in "dead-end jobs" or who "can't settle down." Our paths are all our own, and I am not here to tell you that your job or relationship status are wrong in any way. This is all up to you.

These are just specific examples I often see, and you may be totally different - even in the opposite scenarios. I'm not here to judge! But it all starts with some good old self-reflection. What do you truly want out of life? It's not up to your friends, your boss, or that one family member who thinks they know what's best for you. You are an adult and you - *only you* - have authority over your own life. You would be surprised how many people need to hear that. You may even be surprised to find that you actually needed to hear it, too! Don't let the fear of judgment block you from chasing that aspiration - no matter how wild it may seem to some. People have done crazier things, I'm sure, (just think back to Thomas Edison!) and often have an interesting and fulfilling life doing so.

So many of us see the likes of the world's favorite inventors, writers, performers, and political change-makers and think *wow - aren't they really something.* And they have, of course, made outstanding achievements. Notice I say that their *achievements* are outstanding, but they are just regular people who had doubts, insecurities, and obstacles - just like you. It was their self-efficacy that they got a handle on -and this is what makes all the difference.

Self-Acceptance: The Finishing Line

But wait - here's one last very important term. Self-acceptance alludes to a more all-encompassing affirmation of the self. It requires all of the above areas of self-respect to be fulfilled.

When you're self-accepting, you're able to embrace all facets of yourself—not just the positive, more "marketable" parts. As a result, self-acceptance is unconditional and not subject to the ebbs and flows of our achievements. We can cultivate an awareness of our weaknesses or limitations, but this awareness in no way interferes with our ability to completely accept ourselves.

Everyone faces individual challenges - maybe yours are your fear of public speaking. Or maybe it's maths that's not your strong point, which makes you feel like the laughing stock of your workplace. But for everything you struggle with, I guarantee that there is a strength attached to it. If you struggle with public speaking, for example, you are probably a great listener and known for being humble and sensitive to others' emotions. (This is why it's so overwhelming when all eyes are on you). And if it's maths that sets your head in a spin, then you are likely more on the literal side - and shine brightest when given verbal or communicative tasks. Hey, we can't be naturally gifted at absolutely everything - and that's okay.

We simply need to recognize our strengths and reach our flow-state to realize (in both senses of the word) our true potential, ensuring that our lives and passions are in line.

What is a "flow-state" I hear you ask? Known colloquially as being *"in the zone"* - this refers to the mental state in which a person performing a task is fully immersed in a feeling of energized focus, full involvement, and natural enjoyment. You know, when you're completely absorbed in that one activity that gives you goosebumps and makes you feel invincible? It may be painting, playing an instrument, or solving crossword puzzles - or maybe you haven't found yours yet. But once you acknowledge your core skills and passions that somehow completely immerse you and feel as natural as breathing, you learn to brush over the fact that you struggle at other things.

And this doesn't mean writing off public speaking or maths altogether! There are many challenges we must face that don't feel so natural to us - either due to professional requirements, or simply because you naturally - and rightfully - yearn to push your boundaries. Although, by definition, this isn't easy, it is a remarkably positive exercise. We all must continue to challenge ourselves throughout our lives to push our limits. But don't beat yourself up about it if it takes you a while or you fail a few times. Simply remind yourself of all of those things which you can do rather spectacularly - and that you are not defined by your struggle with this particular challenge. I stress this because while I advocate acceptance of one's "weaknesses," I still wholeheartedly encourage you to push yourself to plow on with what you find the most difficult too, safe in the knowledge that you won't take any setback to heart. The very fact that you accepted this challenge that you know isn't your strongest suit should feed your self-confidence.

And so, strive to know who you really are - what makes you tick, and what you find more testing. You'll feel more in touch with yourself and more fulfilled in everything you do - whether it falls into the former or latter category. You will have the confidence to put yourself out there when it comes to those challenges you know are in perfect alignment with your strengths. But at the same time, you will rise to challenges that lie on the opposite side of the spectrum with this newfound ambitious yet self-accepting approach.

Understanding Self Confidence: Some Final Thoughts

I regularly tell my clients that if they genuinely want to improve their self-esteem and self-confidence, they need to know what parts of themselves they have not yet felt able to accept.

The key lessons to take away from this chapter?

Ultimately, our journey to self-acceptance has many different components, which I hope you now have an improved awareness of.

No one can make you feel inferior without your consent. If you accept yourself, then that's all that matters. That is to say, it's only when we stop judging ourselves that we can secure a more positive sense of who we are. Self-confidence, and thus self-esteem, improve naturally as soon as we cease being so hard on ourselves.

And lastly, self-confidence and self-efficacy are both vital components to your self-esteem. Just as self-esteem is vital for overall self-acceptance. This pyramid-like structure of our self-worth is essential to come to terms with when it comes to not only understanding - but also learning to love and accept unconditionally - our inner self.

Training No. 1
Get to know yourself: Identifying your strengths and weaknesses

Self-confidence isn't about believing yourself to be the best at everything. The people who go around claiming that, in my experience, actually tend to be the most insecure of all. This is because their self-worth depends on what *you* think of them, so they project this seemingly perfect and confident persona. Instead of falling into that trap, try to acknowledge both your strengths and your current weaknesses.

Notice I say "current," because any weaknesses you have are simply due to a lack of training, awareness, or even interests. They aren't a permanent character flaw. You may not yet have learnt to master a skill - or never have any intention to - and that's okay. We all have skills we wish to invest time and energy into mastering - and no one can master everything anyway. It is accepting this that is the first step to truly owning your strengths and feeling confident enough to admit when you are more out of your depth - but to give it your best shot anyway!

So to get the ball rolling, I now ask you to complete the following quick exercise:

Identify 5 of your main strengths and 5 weaknesses - i.e. - 5 things that you currently struggle with or feel less confident doing.

Having it all written down should help you to acknowledge yourself as a full package, and not the two-dimensional caricature we tend to project in our professional - or even personal - lives.

Get to know yourself

Your top 5 strenghts:

- ....
- ....
- ....
- ....
- ....

Uncover your inner strenghts:

What was the most successful task or job I ever fulfilled, and what made me successful?

When faced with an overwhelming obstacle, what's my "go to" skill to overcome it?

What are the strengths that others acknowledge in me?

What skills would I like to build but have not yet had the opportunity to practice?

Your top 5 weaknesses:

- ....
- ....
- ....
- ....
- ....

Uncover your inner weakness:

When faced with an overwhelming obstacle, what's most likely to cause me to give up?

Which weaknesses came up over and over again?

Which weaknesses might hold me back from getting where I need to go?

What are the weaknesses that others acknowledge in me?

3 weaknesses to turn into strenght:

Weakness	How to improve it	Why?
....	....	....
....	....	....
....	....	....

Redeem your bonus!

Hi!

Sorry for the interruption, I truly hope that you are enjoying the book.

I just wanted to tell you that purchasing "Self-confidence training" you have access to my pdf training.

I created these worksheets in pdf so you can download and print them - it is impossible to write on a screen! It will allow you to keep track of your improvements and if you need to redo them in the future.

Download your PDF!

In addition, I will send you some interesting facts and myths about self-confidence by e-mail, don't let go away this opportunity!

Well, thank you for your time and now let's pick up where we left off!

Chapter 2

Setting goals is your road to the life you want

Now that you're set with the definitions and key areas you need to improve on to achieve self-acceptance, let's delve deeper into the actions you can take to set your strengths in motion in order to get there: your goals. Goal-setting is an essential tool for motivation and self-confidence – both in personal and professional contexts. It gives meaning to your day-to-day and fortifies your activities and efforts with the intention of achieving something more.

By setting goals, we essentially lay out a roadmap of where we want to be heading in order to become the version of ourselves we aspire to be. But we must remember to include a plan of how exactly to get to that point. The more thought and detail we put into this plan, the better are our chances of achieving what we aim to.

Just Keep Swimming (By Setting Goals)

If you're one of those people who never fail to show up - whether that is to the office, the gym, or your Italian class

- but fails to truly put their mind to the task at hand and challenge themselves to achieve more each day - then it could be goals that you are lacking. It takes more than just showing up to achieve the big stuff in life. You need ample motivation and determination. And this, you will find, truly flourishes when your self-confidence levels are suitably replenished.

I like to use the analogy of a shark. Hear me out!

Did you know that a shark is so heavy that if it ever stops swimming, even while it's asleep, then it sinks? This would inevitably cause issues. And so a shark never stops swimming its entire life. We can learn a thing or two from our gilled friends. If you are constantly looking towards your next milestone and nudging ever-closer towards your next goal - then you are much less likely to "sink" into that state of self-doubting apathy, many of us know only too well.

The Psychology of Goal-Setting

Goal-setting, from a psychological perspective, refers to the plan of action that we set for ourselves - either consciously or subconsciously. The E-E-E Model is a psychological approach to goal-setting that illustrates how it can affect your self-confidence and self-efficacy. In summary, it teaches that goal-setting improves overall confidence by serving three purposes:

- Enlightening Us. By providing meaningful insight into our abilities and weaknesses, and by helping us shape our goals depending on our own needs.
- Encouraging Us. By providing the motivation and courage to implement our goals to execute our plans efficiently.
- Enabling Us. Goal-setting requires us to achieve a balance between our real and ideal self. By definition, you are identifying an area of your life or abilities that have room for improvement - and taking action. And so, by setting, working towards, and ultimately achieving our goals, we regain self-awareness, self-confidence, and the ability to evaluate and take control over our achievements.

Furthermore, a pioneer in the field of goal-setting Edwin A. Locke, found that professionals in his study who had "highly ambitious" goals had a better performance and output rate than those who didn't. Essentially, this suggests that the bigger your dreams are, the more you will push yourself and thus the better you will perform. But of course, it isn't always so simple. Oftentimes we set goals for ourselves, and they are later forgotten or abandoned.

Why is it that so many of us struggle to follow through with our goals? So much so, that even the mention of "goal-setting" may now fill you with dread - as you associate it with past experiences of disappointment. Indeed, setting a goal only to fail will likely only be damaging to your level of self-confidence. So how can we become better goal-setters?

Learning to Dissect your Goals:

Goals as Easy as "ABC"

Just like when you started school, your commencement into the wonderful world of goal-setting also starts with your ABCs. There are three essential features of goal-setting to begin with, aptly called the "A-B-C" of goals. To put it simply, effective goals must be:

A - Achievable

B - Believable

C - Committed

SMART Goals

Furthermore, goal-setting as a psychological tool for increasing productivity involves five rules, known as the S-M-A-R-T criteria. *(Consider this the high school of goals, now you've passed elementary!)* George T. Doran coined this list in 1981, and it is by far one of the most popular propositions within the psychology of goals.

S-M-A-R-T goals stand for:

S (Specific) – The goal targets a particular area of functioning and focuses on building it.

M (Measurable) –The results can be measured quantitatively or at least indicated by some qualitative attributes. This helps in monitoring the development after executing the plans.

A (Achievable) – The goal is individualized and bespoke to your personal situation. It acknowledges the fact that no single rule suits all.

R (Realistic) – The goal is practical and planned in a way that makes it easy to implement into your own life.

T (Time-bound) – An component of time makes the goal more focused. It also provides a timeframe for the task achievement, making you much more likely to see it through.

Even "SMARTER" Goals

Ready to head to a higher level, still? While SMART marks the alleged golden rules of goal-setting, researchers have also since added two more elements to it, and call it the S-M-A-R-T-E-R rule.

These last two little letters carry an essential function:

E (Ethical) – The interventions and achievements follow professional and personal values.

R (Rewarding) – The end-results of the goal-setting comes with a positive recompense and brings a feeling of success to the user.

Without these last two components, your goals lack depth and may not align with your personal values and motivations. So once you ensure that your goals are "SMART," make them even smarter by asking yourself how they sit with your ethics and a personal sense of purpose.

Your Goals should Involve your Values

As such, effective goals are those, you base on high values and ethics. You must understand your own core values before embarking upon setting goals destined for success. Researches have shown that the more we align our core values and principles with our goals and aspirations, the more likely we are to feel committed to them and to then make them a reality.

Goal-Setting: Self-Confidence and Self-Efficacy

Goals play a key role in how we see ourselves and others. For example, a person who is focused and goal-oriented is likely to have a more positive approach towards life overall, as they are used to constantly looking to the future with hope and positivity. This person is fuelled by their aspirations and self-efficacy and feels self-confident as a result. They perceive any failures as the temporary setbacks they truly are, rather than evidence of inadequacy. And they keep swimming no matter what.

Tony Robbins, a world-famous motivational speaker, and coach once said that "*setting goals is the first step from turning the invisible to visible,*" and I have to agree with him on this one. Setting goals is like building doors between the present and your desired future self. The framework is built and the intention is set, but you still have to then actually open that door and walk through it. Building the door is the necessary starting point - but don't go round hammering at pieces of wood aimlessly and not following through with your intention. Instead, set manageable goals and commit to them. Otherwise, you may feel suitably busy setting the foundations for all of these possibilities - but you can't skirt over the final step - or these good intentions become obsolete.

Goals that Bind You to Reality

We become conscious of our strengths and weaknesses and choose actions that are in line with our capacities.

For example, a committed opera singer most likely doesn't aspire to open a Michelin-star restaurant, while a high-level chef doesn't usually try their luck on the stage. Neither of these hypothetical individuals are better than the other - they just have different skills and have pursued different paths. As such, it is only natural that they set different goals. The important thing is that their own goal is a fine match for their specific skills, efforts, and who they set out to be.

You may, I realize, not be so easily put into a box as an opera singer or chef. However, the need to align your skill to your goal remains the same. Perhaps it will take you a little time to figure out what your "calling" or "flow state" really is. *What will the vessel of your success and ticket to a fulfilled life be?*

However, with adequate self-reflection to identify your strengths (this, I hope you will have made some progress within the previous chapter), followed by ensuring your specific goals are "SMARTER", and you maintain the grit and commitment to them, your self-confidence will sky-rocket, and your life becomes putty in your hands. It doesn't just *happen to you* - you happen to *it*!

So look back at your strengths identified in the last chapter's exercise and incorporate these into your goal-setting. How can you incorporate these characteristics into the future you desire? Realizing our skills and accepting them is a vital aspect of goal-setting as it makes room for self-examination and helps in setting realistic expectations from ourselves.

Goals Require Self-Evaluation

Similarly, goal-setting requires you to really look at yourself – rather than only through the often cloudy lens of others' perspectives. In other words – stop viewing yourself as others may see you and instead learn to self-evaluate directly.

The successful accomplishment of goals is a clear enough indicator that we are doing well. We shouldn't yearn for validation from others on top of that. This is a commitment you make with yourself, for yourself. The fulfillment of which you only hold yourself accountable for. As such, once you reach these goals, set for the right reasons, and upon the right foundations, the satisfaction and self-confidence boost you receive will be more gratifying than any external praise.

The mastery of self-evaluation boosts self-confidence and self-efficacy – as you learn to hold yourself accountable but also to recognize your own successes – separate from anyone else's gaze. This also gives you the motivation to continue setting practical goals or yourself in all future stages of life.

Types Of Goals

All this talk of goals – but what are yours? All goals are different and require different sacrifices and efforts from you to achieve. So now let's take a look at the different types of goals you could have, to shed some light on how to approach them. There are three main types of goals:

Process Goals

Process goals strive towards the realization of plans - they focus on the steps you must take to reach your eventual goal. For example, an hour on the treadmill each morning, writing one chapter of your work-in-progress each day or reading a new book each month. Repeating the same action in a structured way like this is a process goal. The focus is the formation of a new habit that will ultimately lead to achievement.

Performance Goals

Performance-based goals are based on tracking progress and give us a reason to keep going when the going gets tough. These often come with a timeframe, for example: studying for at least 2 hours or exercising for at least 30 minutes per day can help us to regulate our efforts and thus measure our progress in manageable chunks. Maybe you want to gradually increase these efforts, or maintain this level of performance for a set period of time. Either way, these goals help you to push yourself to improve the skill in question, nudging you ever-closer to that sweet final destination.

Outcome Goals

Last but not least: outcome are goals that depend on the successful implementation of your process and performance goals. They keep your perspective in check and help you to keep your eye on the bigger picture. Examples of outcome goals could include shedding a specific amount of weight, learning a new piece on the piano, or qualifying for that promotion.

Which of these resonates most with you? Most likely, you have a combination of goals in mind at any given time. Often our goals are connected with others. Now let's take a look at some more specific and very common types of goals to look deeper into the psychology behind them.

Goals to Change a Habit

A habit is a regular or routine action, over which you feel limited control. Just as we can adopt bad habits unintentionally – such as smoking or biting your nails – we can also teach ourselves new and productive ones. Since habits are, by definition, regular in occurrence, they are relatively quick to develop – as long as you stick to them!

The timeframe required to develop a new habit or routine, depending on its complexity, is usually 3 to 6 weeks. In other words, if you persist with your habit consistently for 3 to 6 weeks, it will become second-nature to you – and thus increasingly challenging to break.

Kicking an old habit takes the same amount of time. In other words, if you don't make your 'habit' at all for a 3 to 6 week period, then after this time it should be much easier to resist, as you have broken the cycle. But kicking some habits is a little harder - such as those that include addictive substances or behaviours. Once you are addicted to something - whether it's smoking, chocolate, or checking your phone - you experience the satisfaction on a biological level. Essentially, you have rewired your own body to "need" you to continue this behavior. So don't scold yourself if you find it hard to master - you are attempting to deny yourself of what your body sees as a basic survival instinct. The key here is will-power, determination, and support.

Just remember that the result will be worth the sacrifice - no pain, no gain, so they say!

Goal to Learn a New Skill

Learning a new skill takes much longer than forming a habit. As a general rule, it takes around 1000 hours to even become "proficient" at a new skill. But this also depends on your existing abilities and where the skill fits in with those you already have. For instance, learning Portuguese is a lot easier for those who already speak Spanish.

To really master a new skill, will most likely take a lot longer than 1000 hours. However, 1000 hours of dedicated practice will give you a good grasp of the skill in question, as well as ample motivation to continue.

Outcome Goals

Outcome goals tend to take the longest time to achieve, as they involve a journey to get there. This could include becoming a partner at your firm, the headteacher at your school, or a professor in your field. Alternatively, it could be buying your dream property or writing a novel.

These goals may take years or even an entire lifetime to achieve. But don't let this make you lose heart - these goals mean you have to be in the long game, but the reward at the end will match your efforts. These aren't a quick-fix or spontaneous stab at a new challenge, but must be backed up by an entire life plan. The high level of commitment required makes it all the more important to establish early on your goal's ABCs - as well as verifying that it passes the SMARTER test.

Once all looks good, so that this lengthy process doesn't become too overwhelming, you should punctuate this journey with milestones that all work up to this eventual goal.

The Importance of Timeframe

Whatever category your goals fall under, setting realistic timeframes is a fundamental first step. How long should it take to achieve your goal? Well, how long is a piece of string? Setting a realistic timeframe depends on so many things. For instance:

Precisely what the goal is – is it just forming a new habit, or does it require learning a new skill?

Is the goal compatible with you? For instance, your intelligence preferences, behavior profile, and motivational needs, or is it going to be more complicated?

Is it a short, medium, or long-term goal? Have you tried to break down your goals into mini-goals and milestones?

What is your level of natural energy and determination?

What resources are needed? For instance, how much time, energy, or money needs to be applied to help you achieve the goal, and do you have them?

What other tasks do you have? What else in your life is currently competing for these resources? If your goal is related to your work, then it may be raising kids that divides your attention. If your goal is related to a hobby or side-hustle, then you need to take your day-job into consideration. Overall, we all must divide our resources - it is possible, as long as we are realistic and sensible in our approach.

Tips on How to Set Goals (And Achieve Them!)

Three Steps To Successful Goal-Setting

Okay, so you get why goals are so vital for your journey to self-confidence and self-acceptance. We understand the importance of timeframe, as well as their overall alignment with our skills, resources, and values. So - where to begin? How do you turn your abstract hopes into concrete goals for your own life?

<u>Make a solid plan</u>

The first step to successful goal-setting is a meticulous plan. Lay out your goals based on your personal strengths, aspirations, and affinities, using the guidelines offered earlier in the chapter as a base. The plan makes your new habit formation easier, as you will have already established where to focus and how to implement the actions.

<u>Make yourself accountable</u>

As touched upon, another essential requirement of goal-setting is accountability. We tend to perform better when someone is watching over us, so it is easier to stick on a diet or skip the gym when no one else is around. But if you learn to become your *own* severe evaluator - you can't ever hide from the observation that's pushing you to continue.

Incorporate rewards and feedback

Rewarding ourselves for our struggles and achievements makes sticking to the plan much easier. Managers who regularly implement feedback to their employees have better performance in their teams than ones who don't. And so, as though you're your own manager, you should take note of your particularly hard work or special milestones and allow yourself to feel proud. Take frequent breaks, and know when it is time to rest. Working non-stop will have the opposite effect on your long-term productivity than you may hope! You wouldn't expect someone else to work under such conditions, after all.

Your goals need to be in line with you

Remember in Chapter 1, where we explored the various areas of self-discovery, with the ultimate goal of self-acceptance? Well, when you are setting goals in your life, this self-acceptance and awareness of your every quirk is crucial. Rather than copy-pasting goals from blogs you see online or indeed, like this one - you have to specifically tailor your goals to align with your strengths, weaknesses, and specific needs and aspirations.

It's no use committing to waking up at 5 am to press weights for 2 hours before breakfast like that bodybuilder on Instagram if you have never set foot in a gym before and merely want to improve your overall health. Or deciding you want to quit all social media because your friend said it helped their mental health if for you, connecting with others online has helped you through darker times and gives you a sense of community. Everyone is different - some need to take a step back and breathe while others need to give themselves a metaphorical kick to get moving. Some of us need to be more humble and listen better to others, whereas some of us need to learn to put ourselves first and to speak up when we feel compelled to.

As mentioned before, self-confidence is all about balance, and there is more than one way to be off-kilter. There is no one-size-fits-all to become a better person - not only because we are all different to begin worth - but also because this notion of a "better person" is subjective anyway - and we all have different ideas of how we want to be.

So find your own balance. Think about what changes to your current habits may do you good and help you do better for those around you. It can be hard to look at yourself objectively in this way, but I encourage you to try. It can be very helpful to imagine what you would think of yourself from an outside perspective - how would you appear? Standoffish? Loud? Warm? Cold?

Surely, there will be some positive and some negative aspects - well, you can't change exactly how others think of you as this largely depends on their own perspectives - but you have full authority over the output you provide. And if this is the way you truly want to come across - whatever that entails - then this is a fundamental part of self-confidence - as you live out your true authentic self. You finally become your own personal manifestation of how a person should be. And this can seep through on a deeper level to impact your more stable level of self-esteem.

Focus on what you want to accomplish

We can easily become overwhelmed with our constantly accumulating inventories of tasks. One of the most effective ways to stay on top of your never-ending to-do list is to keep the bigger picture of your long-term goals in mind. Once you have a clear and overarching picture of what you want to accomplish and for what eventual purpose, you can keep referring back to these bigger picture goals as motivators. That way, if you find that your present burden isn't actually aligned with your overall bigger picture, you can stop yourself from wasting time and energy on struggles that don't form a part of this plan. Here's a great hack I like to use when there's too much on my plate, and I'm not sure where to start. Make a list of all the tasks that need to get done, and see how many of them you can cross off using the 4Ds method below:

The 4 Ds Method

Delay – Sometimes, delaying a niggling task can actually be the more efficient way to ultimately achieve your goals. It may simply free up space on your schedule for more urgent tasks, or allow you to combine this task with something related or that can be done in parallel later on. When a task isn't too time-sensitive, allowing yourself to consciously put it on the back burner can be a lifesaver for both your performance and your mental health. This isn't the same as procrastination, which is avoiding a task you know you need to do. Rather, like you are your own manager, you are deciding to prioritize something else for now, and have a plan in advance of when to start this other thing. Many cases of burnout can be prevented with this simple exercise of planning out which tasks don't actually need to be carried out right away. It helps no one to dive straight into everything as it will only make everything take longer and be of worse quality. Not only that – but you will emerge feeling so drained that it will negatively impact your next tasks too.

Delete – In some cases, delaying certain tasks in this way actually causes them to be obsolete or irrelevant by the time their allocated attention comes around. You realize that it didn't really need to be done at all – as your completion of the preceding tasks means that the item is already sorted or simply isn't even an issue anymore. This is a fantastic feeling! Not only did you manage to complete your other tasks with more precision due to your strategic delaying, but now you can actually cross off an item or two from your to-do list because the problem solved itself. Win!

Delegate – This is a tricky one as it greatly depends on what both your goal and this particular task are, your current circumstances, but also – your self-confidence. Many individuals in managerial roles need to better learn how to decide whether a task absolutely has to be done by themselves, or if it is something that can be delegated to a subordinate or colleague. Many of us see it either as a cop-out (*"I really ought to do this myself,"*), a risk (*"but what if they don't do it right?"*) or simply like an unnecessary burden (*"they probably have other things to do. I shouldn't add this to their load,"*) depending on your personality type as well as on your status and professional relationships in your workplace. But more often than not, passing on certain tasks will not only lighten your load and allow you to perform to a much higher standard with your essential items, but it will also most likely give your coworkers the sense that you trust and approve of their work, and therefore strengthening your working relationships. They may be grateful for the opportunity to try something new, or simply glad of the variety you are adding to their work. Of course, this all depends on many factors - but it's worth considering!

Diminish - This one is simply a combination of all of the above - with the end goal of diminishing your present workload, and thus improving your overall performance. Diminish your area of focus, and you will likely feel more motivated and confident about the more narrow and specialized scope of your work.

Setting Goals: Some Final Thoughts

Now you should know yourself much better - or at least be better equipped with the methods in which to start your journey of self-discovery. Your strengths and weaknesses, your short-term and long-term goals, and the different aspects of self-worth to be nourished and worked upon. So the next point is to fix your goals - to ensure that they are achievable, in alignment with your skills and values, and set within a suitable timeframe.

Goals should motivate you, strengthen your self-confidence levels, and lead to a fulfilling outcome. Reaching small goals will help you out to gain more confidence to achieve the bigger ones. Rather than becoming overwhelmed with an unrealistic stack of tasks in front of you, train yourself to use the 4Ds method in order to handle stressful situations efficiently and, wherever possible, as a team.

Training No. 2
Get started setting goals

Time for our next training exercise. I'm hoping all this talk of goals has made one or two of your own come to mind. Have you ever really sat down and actively thought about your goals – are they achievable? Are they believable? Are you committed to them?

What is the timeframe? And what resources do you need? There's no time like the present to lay all this out to get a better idea of how solid your goals are, and whether the goals themselves need extra work before you can commit to them.

Here's an example answer from yours truly to get you started:

"I would love to leave my current job and change my life; I want to go abroad and live in France
for a few years."

This is my main goal (I have IDENTIFIED the goal), and maybe I could give myself one year to achieve it. It is a goal regarding MYSELF. The problem is that, as you may know, it is usually not so easy to make such a drastic life change. There are always other goals leading up to this it.

First of all, I don't speak French - so my smaller goal would have to be to learn French so I can communicate with people when I arrive in my chosen country - and it will be easier to find a job. This time, my smaller goal is about my work: the TIMEFRAME will be 6 months. And for sure, I will need some money to buy the French course - around $1000, let's say. This, I will write in the RESOURCES box.

Get the idea? Okay, you're turn.

Get started setting goals

Divide the big goals into smaller ones! ↓

Try to find goals for every aspect of your life! ↓

Try to set a realistic and reasonable timeframe. Is it a daily, weekly or monthly goal? ↓

What do I need for reaching my goal? ↓

Identify your goal	Self, relationship or work?	Timeframe	Resources, course or training needed

Chapter 3

You can, you should, and if you're brave enough to start, you will

The most straightforward way to switch to this self-confident, self-accepting, and goal-setting master that you know is bursting to get out? Positive thinking, my friend.

A simple mindset shift can completely transform your inner-strength and capacity to cope with whatever lies ahead. So when your life becomes overwhelming, and you're not sure how to process it, remember the ever-relevant stoic mode of thinking that despite the fact you can't always control what goes on *outside* of yourself, you have complete authority over what happens within your own mind - even though it may not feel that way at times!

Trust me - you will find it a massive release to let go of your anxieties over what you simply cannot control. It may be genuinely terrible - the bad health of a loved one, a natural disaster, or a certain global health crisis...

Of course, you can't simply switch off your concern for these problems. It's not that simple - you're not a robot. However, rather than falling into the all-too-common trap of obsessing and wallowing in the aspects outside of your control, it can be a lot less damaging - not to mention more productive - to shift your focus over to how you *can* take action.

As Epictetus put it:

"What really frightens and dismays us is not external events themselves, but the way in which we think about them. It is not things that disturb us, but our interpretation of their significance."

You may not be able to cure an illness, but you can help the person in need. You may not be able to reverse a natural disaster or solve a global crisis, but you can find ways to help your community and take positive steps to piece your life back together. Life has its challenging moments, but the key is in how you react and respond to them. This will not only give you the motivation to "keep swimming," but will give you more of a handle on your life and emotions, which will help to solidify your self-confidence as well as your self-esteem in the longer term.

Is your glass half-empty or half-full?

Although perhaps an overused analogy, how you instinctively answer this age-old question when faced with real-life scenarios says a great deal about your overall outlook on life, your attitude toward yourself, and ultimately - your self-confidence.

Positive thinking is key here - but that doesn't mean keeping your head buried in the sand! Rather, it is a question of approaching the challenges in your life in a different, more productive way. You hope for the best outcome, but you are nonetheless emotionally prepared for the worst.

For this to work, a positive inner-monologue - in other words, the way that you talk to yourself - is fundamental. If your thoughts are overwhelmingly negative, then your entire outlook on life and your own self-worth will follow suit. On the other hand, if your internal musings are more positive, your entire perception of the world and your place in it will follow suit.

If you're a self-confessed pessimist, though, you can still learn to turn your negative ruminations into more positive affirmations. The process is simple, but like all the valuable skills in life, it can take time and practice — you're implementing a new habit, after all.

How to Embrace a Growth Mindset

We all feel more positive some days than others. It would be unrealistic to expect yourself never to have negative thoughts again, or to be happy no matter what. The truth is that challenges will always lie ahead - this is unavoidable. However, by adopting an overall more positive and growth-focused mindset, you can retain a baseline of positivity no matter what turbulent times may lie ahead. By acknowledging that you will inevitably have difficult times ahead, you become less fearful. You can't control this fact, and worrying now will not make things any easier later - so you may as well enjoy every moment and tackle each issue as it comes.

Just as you must come to terms with your alleged weaknesses in skill and character to have a more fulfilling enjoyment of your strengths, the same applies to areas of your life. You shouldn't refuse to acknowledge the painful parts, but you shouldn't ruminate over them either. It takes a lot of inner-strength, but we must learn to acknowledge, accept, and move past these negative parts of our life. Ignoring negativity won't get us anywhere.

So how can you part ways with your negative, self-sabotaging behaviors and move towards a mindset of growth and positivity? Here are some pointers to get you started:

Immerse yourself in positivity

Make an effort to spend most of your precious jours with positive people who you can count on to support you and lift you up instead of dragging you down. At times, we all need to lend an ear to a suffering loved one, but overly negative people can drain your energy, motivation, and self-confidence levels while fanning the flames of stress and self-doubt. The same goes for your entertainment and content consumption: from the books and articles you read to the music you listen to — everything you expose yourself to has an impact on the overall outlook you have on your life— so take back control over this. Be conscious of what you read and watch just as who you engage with - it's for the sake of your own mental wellbeing and inner-strength.

Positive self-talk

To feed this refreshingly positive outlook, try following this one life-changing rule: *Treat yourself as you would any loved one in your life.* Be as supportive and forgiving in your internal monologues as you would towards a dear friend or relative opening up to you about a problem or mistake. And if a negative thought threatens to shake up this inner peace and self-acceptance, then consider, how would you feel if someone spoke about your best friend in that way? Defend your worth as you would somebody else's. You owe it to yourself, and your self-esteem will thank you.

Practice gratitude

Each day, make an effort to acknowledge what you have going for you and what there is to be grateful for. This simple act alone of recognizing whatever may be in your favor — be it your friendships, your family, or your current state of health — the blessings many people lest we forget, are craving. Conscious awareness of the abundance of fortune in your life in the present moment is essential for maintaining this growth mindset. Please don't succumb to the toxic temptation of only blinkering yourself towards what you *do not* yet have or what you *cannot* yet do.

Stop spiraling

Train yourself to stop and evaluate what you're thinking periodically throughout each day. If you find that you tend to assume the very worst and base your attitude on this habit, then discover ways to turn these negative thought processes on their head. Remind yourself that, come what may, you have already proven yourself to be strong and intelligent countless times, and you can face it. Whatever you may have shown outwardly in the past, you know - and only you - what you are truly capable of. You simply need the confidence to project this potential externally - and that is what you are now preparing yourself to do. Overall, no matter what someone else may think about you, as long as you can get behind your own decisions values, you can, and will, succeed. Hold onto these affirmations internally, and you will rein in that tendency to spiral into panic at the hint of any upcoming obstacle.

Move your body

Physical exercise has been proven time and time again to elevate a persistent low mood and reduce stress levels significantly, so it's important you force yourself to move your body - even when you really don't feel like it! Once the blood and endorphins start pumping, you will feel some immediate positive effects, and it will become increasingly easier to maintain a positive mindset. But don't get me wrong - you don't have to be an athlete or bodybuilder to feel the post-exercise self-confidence boost. Whether it's just a walk in the park or a high-power work-out, the feeling that you are taking control over your body to strengthen it not only makes you feel mentally stronger, too - but it helps to shift your mindset to one of growth and energy. Exercising is perhaps the most reliable way to get an instance self-confidence boost.

Don't forget to laugh!

Lastly, give yourself permission to smile, laugh, and see the funny side - even during difficult times. Break out of that tunnel-vision feeling when something negative is on your mind. You don't have to only think about that - it won't help you or anyone else. Even if you can't avoid thinking about something completely, it's important to give your mind a well-deserved break. When you can laugh at life, it seems a whole lot less intimidating!

The Law of Attraction

You may well have heard of the law of attraction. The new phrase circulating the internet lately is receiving an intensely polarised response. Some people interpret it as a spiritual or even a supernatural phenomenon. However, for others - myself included - it is merely a concise way of explaining how life curiously seems to deliver exactly what we project for ourselves.

For instance, if you push through each day of a job you hate imagining yourself in a more desirable role, and channeling your efforts into this dream - one day, you are likely to make this aspiration a reality. But if you convince yourself that this is your fate, and there's no point pushing for anything more, then what chance do you have? Similarly, children who are consistently lifted up and told they are clever and will do great things by their parents and teachers tend to do very well at school. Fuelled by the praise and external confirmations of their competence, they see themselves as good students, and that is what they become. On the other hand, a child who is consistently told throughout their school career that they are stupid and won't achieve anything, sadly, begins to believe it. And so, this projection of themselves as an underachiever often becomes a reality.

The "Law of Attraction" essentially boils down to this: Once we believe ourselves to be failures, or that we have reached our limit and can't hope for more, we stop pushing ourselves. We stop hoping for more and become dangerously comfortable with our current less-than-satisfying reality. I'm not implying that you can have anything you want just by visualizing it, but whether you close yourself off or open up mentally to your possibilities has a profound effect on what you end up achieving.

As such, you must grasp this potential of manifesting your future. Even the most skeptical among us can see that we often end up achieving as much as we believe ourselves capable of - and this works both ways. So don't limit yourself - build yourself up! Even if only within your own mind. Picture yourself doing the job of your dreams, or living in the house you fantasize about, or in the relationship you truly want for yourself. It is only you who can deliver on these ambitions - don't make the mistake of just sitting there, waiting for what you want to come to you.

Studies have even revealed that by training your mind to focus what you want in life - but in a positive rather than self-pitying way - the brain actually, in a sense, *"rewires itself"* to strive for this ideal image, solidifying it as an essential part of your identity. As such, upon achieving the goal, you feel that sense of fulfillment you crave. If we don't, then our brain keeps nudging us until we do. Your brain has that "tough love" thing down to a tee and will hold you accountable to those goals you set for yourself.

In a way, you are creating your reality in every moment of every day. You are shaping your future with every single thought and decision. You can't take a break from it and decide not to create - because this process never stops as long as you live.

Positivity: A Question on Give-And-Take

Similarly, it often helps to project outwardly what you are searching for. Some may call it "manifesting to the universe," which is fine if you see it that way - but if that sounds a little too out-there for you, I simply see it as the give-and-take of positivity. Think about it - in nature, every single organism, from the tiniest cell in your own body to the whales in the ocean and the birds in the skies, have a sort of natural give-and-take system with the world around them. In fact, nothing in this universe is static. Every element of it - including you and I - are constantly in motion, and always giving and taking from the elements around us.

Your tissue cells, for instance, are constantly exchanging oxygen, water, and glucose with surrounding cells. On a larger scale, the earth's many ecosystems depend on the cycle of the animals eating the plants and then giving back the energy after they die and decompose. The plants take in carbon dioxide and release oxygen, while the animals do the opposite.

And so, we also flourish as human beings when a movement or exchange is taking place. We can never be completely independent of our surroundings. Try it for yourself: if you want to receive more joy, start by inspiring joy in others. If love and compassion from others are what you seek, then offer this to those around you. And if you pursue professional success, then support and celebrate the success of your colleagues. This is why selfishness and envy don't help you in the long-term. Life is a two-way street: the more you give, the more you receive.

Body language and hormones
Use Confident Body Language and Attitude

Now here is some solid advice you can incorporate immediately. Body language is one of the most powerful tools that can either make or break your self-confidence. Once you cultivate awareness for how your physical stature and non-verbal signals can influence not only how others perceive you - but how you perceive yourself - there's truly no looking back.

The science of body language can seem off-puttingly complex. But to start with the basics: in the animal kingdom, if you make yourself big, you stretch out, you take up space, you're declaring your power and confidence. And the opposite is a declaration of submission and an admission of weakness. Humans do the same thing - both as a short-term reaction to a fleeting sense of high or low self-confidence and also as a more long-term way of behaving that reflects overall self-esteem. In other words, we may all throw our hands up in the air once we win a game or cross them to our chest when we are being criticized, which reflects our temporary self-confidence - but how do you tend to hold yourself generally speaking? Are your limbs clamped shut and your spine curved, or is your body language open, your spine straight and your head held high? This is how you can get a sense of someone's self-esteem, which, as discussed back in Chapter 1 is our more permanent sense of self-worth.

This behavior is especially interesting because it shows us how universal and unavoidable our expressions of power are. You are always speaking - even when you are silent! Studies show that even those born blind will adapt to these non-verbal cues. For instance, when they cross the finish line of a race, and they've won, it doesn't matter if they've never seen anyone do this, but their arms instinctively fly up in a V-shape, and their chin lifts. It's an animalistic instinct - not just a learned behavior as we previously thought.

So use this to your advantage to change the signals you give out to the world. Imagine you are talking to an outwardly confident person - how do they look? Maybe they sit with their knees open, their palms showing, they make direct eye contact, and they think nothing of extending an arm or leg to lean nonchalantly as they talk to you. Now think of an obviously insecure person in that same chair, they probably cross their legs - maybe their arms too. Or their arms lie limply stuck to their sides, and they clasp their palms together. They avoid direct eye contact and their gaze is lowered in submission. They seem to take up as little space as possible, and their entire body seems closed off - their torso retreats as though they anticipate an attack.

When we feel vulnerable, powerless, or ashamed, we instinctively close up. We wrap ourselves up and make ourselves small. And if someone in our vicinity is asserting power, and we feel we are somehow less worthy of respect (say for example a domineering boss, an abusive partner, or if you have social anxiety, just about anyone!) we tend to make ourselves smaller as a subconscious effort to become less noticeable, and to visibly back down and submit to their alleged authority.

Well - it's about time you stopped that! Even when you are, in a sense, objectively "subordinate" - for instance, if you are conversing with a manager at work, or even at a job interview, you can train yourself to assert power through body language. You may feel small and unworthy inside, but the simple act of sitting up straight with your head held high actually takes a physiological effect on your brain, giving your self-confidence a noticeable boost. In other words - the better you are at "faking" your confidence, the more you will feel the real thing begin to emerge within you.

So think of how a self-confident person would look - how they would sit, talk, walk, or stand to wait for the bus… and try emulating that. You'd be surprised what a difference the exterior your project can make on the inside.

So we know that our minds change our bodies, but is it also true that our bodies change our minds?

All in the Hormones

Powerful people tend to be, perhaps not surprisingly, more assertive, more optimistic, and - you guessed it - more self-confident. They're the ones who feel like they're going to win - even at games of chance. They tend to be able to think more abstractly rather than being consumed by logic. And so they take more risks. And if you were paying attention to the part on visualizing your successes, this can have a huge impact on the individual's success. It really makes you think – does optimism make you powerful, or power make you optimistic? I would argue – for the most part – the former!

That being said, there are also physiological differences regarding two main hormones: testosterone (the dominance and determination hormone) and cortisol (the stress and anxiety hormone.) Before you jump to any conclusions – both women and men do produce testosterone – but the fact that generally speaking, men produce a lot more, is considered a key factor influencing the modern phenomenon of "imposter syndrome" and the ongoing confidence deficit between males and females as early as primary school. This has a noticeable impact on women's attempts to pursue high-level roles in certain fields.

On top of that, some women produce more testosterone than others, just as some men have much higher levels than others. And studies show that the people – whatever their particular gender – who naturally produce more testosterone, tend to be more self-confident, more assertive and more competitive. The power they put out means they receive more power in return.

There is little you can do to change your testosterone levels noticeably. And high levels in women can come with other issues, anyway. But what about the part played by our gender-neutral stress hormone, cortisol? Well, power is also a lot about how you react to stress. Does anyone look for a leader that's dominant but really sensitive to stress? No - you want the person who's powerful, assertive and dominant - but not very stress reactive. The person who's laid back and takes things in their stride. The person who isn't easily frazzled or rattled and who can remain calm and collected when the going gets tough. To be this inspirational vision of calm, you must have low cortisol levels. Here's the good news: you can greatly manipulate your levels of this hormone.

Trying to lower stress levels is the best way to lower cortisol, as it is your stress and anxiety which kick your body into fight-or-flight mode. That's what gives you that heart-pounding, nauseating, muscle-tensing response before a presentation, when you just made a big work mistake, or you are rushing to get an important task done on time. Your body reads your stress as an indicator that a physical threat - such as a predator or a violent competitor - is imminent, and so it prepares the way evolution has taught it to. But this intrinsic response to stress doesn't help much in the context of our modern lives. So although cortisol may have its uses in extreme situations, when this hormone spikes too often, it can have damaging effects. You can't just fight that colleague or run away from the office screaming - and so, this nervous energy accumulated thanks to the cortisol spike goes unused. And your body is punishing you for it, jolting you into a state of terror and physical unease. It means well, though - it believes you are in the grasp of imminent death - and yet you are just sitting there still, at your computer!

By practicing more positive thinking as well as making simple lifestyle changes - such as limiting caffeine, alcohol, and sugar, spending quality time outdoors and away from technology, and getting adequate exercise, sleep, and downtime - you can effectively take action to reduce stress and keep their cortisol levels at a healthier and more manageable level.

And so, our bodies change our minds, our minds change our behavior, and our behavior can change our future.

Become a realistic optimist

Although a positive mindset is essential, it would be counterproductive to believe that hardship doesn't exist, your problems will dissolve, or that your goals will magically be achieved without you taking any action or making any sacrifice. Being a realistic optimist means an awareness of our challenges and an acknowledgment that in order to get what we want, we need to take action.

We focus on the best actions to take under our specific circumstances and yet accept that which is beyond our own control. Try to combine a positive attitude with an honest evaluation of the challenges you may meet along your path. Along with imagining what it is you would like the outcome to be, imagine the steps you will take to overcome the challenges. Expect the unexpected and know that you have the inner tools to deal with unexpected challenges.

Furthermore, don't obsess over the negativity you may currently have in your life. Of course, you shouldn't ignore it either, but don't make it your all-consuming sole focus, or you'll drive yourself mad! As already discussed, a positive mindset can completely transform the way you live. You can go a step further by making use of humor to turn a negative mood or situation on its head. Admittedly, it's not always the time or the place, but I must reiterate how humor can be used to boost your self-confidence and contentment long-term. It provides you with a new and refreshing perspective about your problems and stresses, and stops you from taking yourself too seriously!

Finally, following the basics of self-care can reinforce your inner strength and completely reshape your attitude when faced with a stressful situation—for example, exercise and meditation help to release endorphins, and feed a more positive outlook. Eating and sleeping well are also fundamental for a positive mood and effective brain functioning in general! So don't discount your most basic physical needs just because the source of your stress may seem more important than your yoga class, your dinner, or your bedtime - nothing should trump these daily life rafts that keep us functioning humans at the most basic level.

Positive Thinking: Some Final Thoughts

Positive thinking can truly transform your life in the internal sense: how you perceive yourself, your self-confidence, how you present yourself to others. As a knock-on effect, it also boosts your external endeavors. Call it the "Law of Attraction" or simply a fact of life: if you convince yourself and others that you are able to do something, you will set out the necessary conditions to make it true.

If you struggle with persistent negative thinking and self-flagellating thoughts that limit your ambition and prevent you from reaching your goals, be easy on yourself - but start with this very basic practice of positive thinking. It may not seem like much in the face of all of your life's struggles. You may even find it somewhat offensive to imply you simply need to "cheer up." But that is not it at all. Positive thinking is simply a mindset shift. Although it may be a humble first step, it can eventually transform your self-confidence and self-efficacy - and this will give you that much-needed push in the direction of your goals that you are searching for.

With practice, your inner-voice will soften. It will let go of the self-criticism to make room for self-acceptance. And by becoming more empathetic and accepting of others, as a byproduct of this newfound attitude, you begin to give out into the world what you hope to reap. This can be not-only fulfilling for your own goals, but comes with the gratification that you are also supporting others on their journey to theirs.

I mean, look around — every single person you meet is facing personal challenges and struggles too. Admittedly, there is a huge range in the potential severity of people's personal struggles— but we still shouldn't forget that everyone has their particular trials and tribulations, and burdens to bear, that they face differently. You may not always see it from the outside, so be mindful of how those around you may be facing struggles not so different from your own.

Overall, whatever comes your way, when you tap into that growth mindset and the mental realm of positivity, you're better able to handle everyday stress more constructively and to look to the future with more hope, more empathy, and of course, more self-confidence.

Training No. 3
Positive Thinking and the Growth Mindset

It's time for our next training. For this one, as you may have guessed, the emphasis is on positive thinking. How can you take your existing negative thoughts and transform them with a fresh perspective?

You're out of work? Now you have the perfect opportunity to change your career path to something more in line with your strengths and ambitions. An enforced fresh start that these days are rare to come by.

You just ended a relationship? Well, it may have hurt but now all the negativity that led to the separation can stay in your past. You can now indulge in some much-needed self-reflection and work on your self-confidence as a separate entity to any other person.

You get the idea. Even your most painful of thoughts can have a silver lining if you think enough about it. Even if it is the lessons you can take from this problem, or that you will not make the same mistake again.

Well, what are you waiting for?

Positive Thinking and the Growth Mindset

On the left, write down as many automatic negative thoughts that come into your mind about yourself.
When finished, take the time to challenge every negative thought by finding a positive, truthful replacement and then write it on the right side

Automatic Negative Thoughts	Positive Thought Replacement

By changing your thoughts, you will change the way you feel.

Chapter 4

Facing your fears gives you strength, courage, and confidence

One of the best ways to build self-confidence and to maintain a positive mindset through thick and thin is to accumulate and overcome challenges. Many people mistakenly believe they're confident or upbeat because of their accomplishments. However, in reality, this self-confidence and growth mindset is more a result of the obstacles they overcame to achieve these feats.

If you truly crave self-confidence, success, and fulfillment, you cannot ignore or hide away from your fears. Now is the time to train yourself to break out of your comfort zone - to face your fears and self-imposed limitations and to reach your true potential.

And here's a secret: your potential is a lot greater than you probably think. But from the cozy yet confined bubble of your comfort zone, you may not even be able to see it - let alone reach it.

What is the Comfort Zone?

There's a lot of talk these days about getting out of your comfort zone - but what does that mean exactly? You need to know what a comfort zone is in order to break out of it. And this is very different for everyone. Your comfort zone is essentially a psychological state of familiarity, ease, and control. It is within the bounds of this state where you experience low levels of anxiety and stress, where you feel comfortable and not particularly stretched, and you feel certain that you can handle whatever is on your plate. Sounds great, right?

Although I don't recommend remaining perpetually outside of the limitations of your comfort zone by constantly pushing yourself and never giving yourself a break or maintaining a steady level of effort and performance - as this can cause your anxiety levels to soar and is the reason why so many over-workers now suffer from burnout. This is essentially what happens when you don't stop pushing your limits for too long. This way, you spread yourself too thin, and your exhausted mind and body mean that you lose the spark that initiated your venture anyway. This way of working simply isn't sustainable, and if kept up for too long, you will eventually break - either physically, psychologically, or, indeed, both! You're only human after all.

But this doesn't mean you should shy away from hard work or challenges either. We're all different, and so are our particular challenges - but it's about finding that balance between stepping outside of your comfort zone to push your existing boundaries, but knowing when to rein it in, to pause, to take a break.

In the comfort zone, a steady level of performance is possible, but no more than that. In fact, many people go their whole lives, never breaking out of their comfort zone. This isn't to say that they don't overcome challenges, or that they don't achieve some level of success. But they faced obstacles as they arrived. They didn't head towards the obstacles with intent and a healthy dose of self-confidence to see them through. They achieved things that came relatively easy to them - Or put in effort but only in manageable doses - such as going to university - but only to study something that is relatively easy or connected to a stable job, rather than choosing something which drives and challenges them. Or bagging that not-too-demanding entry-level job after graduating, and then staying put there for the years that follow because it "makes sense." It's what you know. And it pays the bills. Then maybe they finally buy their own place - but in their hometown, as they never saw themself living anywhere else. Why would they? This is familiarity. This is comfort. This is just *easier*, isn't it?

I don't advocate taking the easy route either. Sometimes life just works like that. We may be lucky enough to truly want the path laid out before us and so we must grasp it. However, we all face more turbulent paths throughout life too - and we shouldn't shy away from the slightest chance of effort or difficulty in favor of the easy life. At least - not if we want to maintain a healthy level of self-confidence, self-esteem, and enthusiasm for living.

If your only obstacles in life have been a case of you taking them as they come while avoiding difficulty whenever possible, then this is living passively, my friend. If you are breaking out of your comfort zone and putting yourself out there, throwing yourself in the deep end from time to time - knowing full well that these difficulties lie ahead, but going for it anyway, then your self-confidence levels will soar. You will regain a sense of authority over your future. And I see time and time again that this completely transforms my clients' overall life successes and satisfaction.

Anxiety: Friend or Foe?

Bearing all this in mind, what can we learn from our stress and anxiety? We hear a lot of talk about anxiety these days. It can make you back away from challenges, retreat into yourself, and even physically harm your body, due to the spikes in stress hormones cortisol and adrenaline that it implies. However, did you know that humans actually maximize their performance at elevated levels of anxiety? This is known as the Yerkes-Dodson curve.

You may think this statement is in contradiction of my earlier encouragement to lower your stress and thus, your cortisol levels, but let me explain better. I stand by the fact that chronic stress is not your friend. Long-term high cortisol levels that give you that constant on-the-edge, stomach-lurching nervousness can be seriously damaging. However, as touched upon, this natural response from your body has good intentions. The spike in cortisol leads to a tunnel vision of your threat, a suppressed appetite, lowered libido, a fast heart rate, and a tensing of the muscles. This can all be rather inconvenient when you are in the throes of the average western modern life. And can't switch off from your work worries, lose interest in what used to make you happy, and feel constantly tense and sick to the stomach. But if your threat was a lion in the savannah, these sudden physical changes are what made our ancestors spring into action. The jolt of nervous energy was what gave them the strength to escape. The suppressed appetite and libido meant that their brains weren't distracted by the usual motivations of food and sex, and maintained this intense focus on the danger in question until the threat subsides.

And even today, in small bursts, we can use this anxiety to our advantage. That jittery surge you get when you're in a hurry can actually be just what you need to get the job done. That tunnel-vision feeling you get when you are determined to succeed can help fuel the fire to your success and ensure that you remain committed to your goals. You simply have to make sure that amidst all of this, you learn to switch off. You learn to leave this all-consuming drive at the office, or on the running tracks - wherever your particular breed of success is cultivated. You remember to be present when around family and friends, and to give these thoughts a rest once you are getting ready for bed. Even if you are 100% dedicated to your goal - you can't give it 24 hours of your day. You need adequate rest and downtime to get you there - so make sure that these precious moments aren't sullied by your anxiety-fuelled musings. Learn to switch them off.

So the bottom line is that anxiety has a specific purpose. When it gives the necessary burst of energy and motivation to get something done or to get out of danger - it is literally a life-saver. However, there's nothing natural about the steady stream of anxiety that many of us suffer from today. It's intended as a short term, and not a long-term response. As such, it can lead to both mental and physical health problems. So next time you get that tight-chested jittery feeling, consider why. *Where is it coming from?* And then consider if it is useful to you at this time. If you are in the last 5 minutes before an important deadline or about to cross the finish line of a race, then maybe it will give you what you need. However, if you are simply lying awake at night, socializing with friends, or carrying out non-urgent tasks - then take a deep breath. Remember that this is simply a biological response to your fears. Acknowledge these fears and move past them - however, you need to do that under the specific circumstances.

The Yerkes-Dodson Curve

As touched upon, the Yerkes-Dodson curve suggests that performance and anxiety are directly related. In simple terms, an increase in the stress hormone, cortisol - up to a certain point, of course - can help to boost your performance. Once your anxiety crosses this optimal level, though, your performance will drop pretty spectacularly. So essentially, when it comes to your stress and anxiety levels, you are walking on a knife's edge... (forgive me if this analogy only raises them!)

This idea of a curve was first proposed by psychologists Robert Yerkes and John Dillingham Dodson in 1908. In their experiment, they discovered that rats could be motivated to complete a maze with slight electrical shocks. But, as the shocks increased in power, their performance level decreased significantly, and they just ran around, seeking an escape. It was clear from the experiment that anxiety levels helped to focus attention and motivation on the task at hand, but only up until a certain point.

Next time you feel all over the place with nerves, just think of those rats. Your anxiety levels have crossed the threshold of productivity and now only serve as a biological alarm bell to get you out of harm's way, and fast. Before you continue with the task at hand, you need to take a step back and acknowledge the sensations you are feeling, and how they are actually clouding your vision and harming your performance.

Take a deep breath. You are alive, and you are a human with needs and limits. You are not in danger. You don't need to run anywhere or fight anyone. You need to remain calm and concentrate.

You can complete the task, but only once your mind is clear, your heart rate slows down, and you regain that sense of control over your thoughts and actions. It may be easier said than done, but during this journey to a more self-confident, self-accepting you, you can use this newfound sense of inner peace and security to also be accepting of your natural limitations. You can learn to push yourself when safe and necessary, but also to know when to take a step back for your own good - as well as for the good of your project. It simply takes practice and self-awareness.

Thinking vs. Doing

Hopefully, you'll remember the difference between self-confidence and self-efficacy, as discussed in the first chapter. But just to give you a quick recap: self-confidence is the belief that you *can,* while self-efficacy is the drive to ensure that you *will.* Essentially, it's all well and good to think you can achieve anything you set your mind to - but make sure you do actually "set your mind" to something at some point...

Don't be one of those people who have many plans and goals, simply doesn't follow them through, but then blames the world for it. Sometimes, things happen beyond our control, which hinder our success. Other times, our path is laid out, and the intention is there, but that lingering fear stops us from taking that first significant step. Learn to notice when you are thinking more than you are actually doing. Sometimes, we big ourselves up so much in our mind, imagining all the things we will do, that we forget the important part of actually *doing* things.

What are you afraid of? (Not a rhetorical question!)

I have found that there are three types of fear that damage my clients' self-confidence, and hold them back from achieving their potential:

The fear of Failure - "I can't do it"

If this is the fear that most resonates with you, then it's your self-belief that is the issue. As already discussed at great length, self-confidence is crucial to be able to look at yourself with a positive mindset. To believe in your own abilities, and to push yourself to rise to challenges requires for you to achieve your full potential. If you find yourself letting the defeatist mantra "I can't" invade your inner-monologue, then you must actively try to combat this. Recognise that this is an attitude, and the product of your low self-confidence - but nothing more. And remember that failures are what shape us and spur us on to do more. They shouldn't be something to be fearful of, but merely guides to lead you down the path you need to take - whether it's to try harder or try a different approach - your failures can teach you a lot about how to succeed.

The fear of Criticism - "What will other people think?"

If it's the fear of others' judgment that you find the most potent, then you are still attaching far too much importance to the opinions of those around you. You may have this issue even if you are someone with a relatively high level of self-belief - but this is too easily threatened by the slightest critique or disapproval. As mentioned in earlier chapters, you cannot live your life in fear of what others think about you. Although it's natural to care about how we present ourselves to others, many of us take this too far. We obsess so much about how we are perceived by others that we actually forget how we perceive ourselves. Even if other people truly do see you as less competent than you believe you are - as long as you believe in your own abilities, then that's all that really counts. You can change how you look at yourself, but have no direct control over how others see you. As such, your best bet is to live your life on your own terms - putting your own opinions and ideas before those of others. After all, you are your own person! And no one - no matter how well they may know you - can see the full picture. So don't let the fear of external judgment hold you back!

The fear of Rejection - "What if it's a no?"

Similarly, if you go through life afraid of the word "no" - you will really miss out. Here's the thing: the most worthwhile challenges in life are difficult. They don't come easy. And you can't be sure that you will get the result you want. But that shouldn't be enough to deter you! One "no" shouldn't send you running and hiding, as it does to so many. It shouldn't be the be-all-and-end-all. It is just one negative response - and there are always so many other opportunities out there. I guarantee that whoever your greatest role-model is - and whatever field their success was in - if they gave up after the first "no" - or even the first ten or twenty in most cases - you would not be able to enjoy their contribution to the world today.

This links back to my earlier explanation of self-efficacy - the drive that makes you turn your goal into a reality. If you are quickly put off and take any negative responses to heart, then you may not make it through the journey, However, if your self-efficacy level is high enough for you to take any setbacks on the chin and plow on forward anyway, then this is the real ticket to success. Let go of this fear of people saying "no," - it's only a short word after all - and it's over very quickly! Take this as one door shutting to allow another to open, and move on. Your future self requires it of you!

Be curious, not fearful

Be curious and realize that fear is often based on false or self-sabotaging interpretation. Think of it this way: you cannot experience fear and curiosity simultaneously. Because we cannot feel both scared and curious about something at the same time: our physiology can only be set in one mode out of the two. This means that when we switch *into* "curiosity mode," we naturally move away from fear. And since fear tends to lead us away from rational or positive thinking due to its less-than-pleasant nature, this is probably a pretty good idea...

Try this simple exercise: the next time you feel fearful about something, ask yourself, *"Is there something about this situation I could get curious about?"* Fear often comes up in situations of uncertainty, as we are hardwired to reject the unknown as a survival instinct - but as we all know, once we delve deeper, this is not always justified!

Also, consider this great quote by Bertrand Russell:

"Fear is the main source of superstition, and one of the main sources of cruelty. To conquer fear is the beginning of wisdom."

By overcoming your fears, you are not only on the path to wisdom, you are on the path to success. As already discussed in-depth, self-confidence is fundamental for success. But facing your fears is also essential for self-confidence. It's not a problem to have fears in the first place - we all do. So don't beat yourself up about the personal challenges and worries you face. Simply accept that fear is a fact of life - but so is gathering our courage to face them.

Another thing I want to point out: fear causes inaction. When I find myself procrastinating, I always ask, "What am I afraid of?" and there is *always* something deep-rooted. You may think you are just *really into* that TV series, or simply needed to clean your entire house before attempting the task at hand. But beneath all that naive reasoning, I guarantee you are shrouding a fear somewhere. You may not even realise it yourself. You may truly believe that your reasons for procrastinating are simply superficial. But most likely, you are scared of what will happen if you complete the task and it's bad. What if you channel your efforts into this task, like you're supposed to, and you realize you are just not good enough?

That's why, as a defense mechanism, many of us distract ourselves and put off these duties. It buys us time, but it also gives us a welcome excuse if things don't go so well.

"Ah yes, I really should have spent more time on that! That's why it wasn't my best work."

It gives you a reason for underperforming that is much easier to swallow. However, what if you put in the time and effort that you should have, and produced some truly outstanding work? I guess now, you'll never know. That really is a shame.

Once you identify the fear that's holding you back, you can acknowledge it and take action. Action cures fear, while inaction and procrastination only feeds it...

Dr. Sharon Melnick also suggested that *'...fear manifests itself as a series of "what ifs." "What if I fail?" "What if people criticize me and my ideas?" "What if people reject me?"...'*

According to Dr. Melnick's findings, these "what ifs" hold you back by preventing you from testing your comfort zone. She says, however, that these fleeting fears stop successful people. She wrote:

"Fear is a natural, evolutionary based response to new situations, but what ifs come from your lack of confidence and lack of self-trust. If you don't trust yourself to be able to learn and course-correct from any mistakes, if you don't have a secure feeling that 'no matter what happens, I will make a good situation out of it', *and if you don't have a strong and accurate appreciation of your own value, then you will feel a need to maintain tight control over and pre-forecast the outcomes of any new step…The most successful people, follow the cliché,* 'feel the fear and do it anyway,' *because they have core confidence underneath their fear."*

Just as you shouldn't let success go to your head, you also shouldn't allow failure stop you from trying again. Appreciate your little victories and reap motivation from them. Then learn from your small failures along the way. *How can you do better? How will it be different next time now knowing what you know?* Use those pesky "what ifs" to develop contingency plans, rather than allowing them to stop you in your tracks. And don't focus on what other people think. Instead, focus on your own ideas of how you can improve, learn, grow, and make *yourself* proud. Have faith in your abilities, and don't let the fear of what may be come to get in the way of your plans.

Face Your Fears and Gain Self-Confidence: Some Final Thoughts

So that's my take on how facing your fears and taking the appropriate action can build your self-confidence and empower you to achieve your full potential. But everyone has different fears, different goals, and different capacities - so now it's over to you to figure all of yours out.

Training No. 4
Face Your Fears

It can be surprisingly hard to identify your fears in black and white. However, the most helpful thing in overcoming your fears is to become aware of them. Identify them. See them for what they are. Fear is simply an emotion or feeling that we feel based on the belief that we are in danger. Some fear is healthy such as the fear that comes from seeing a rattlesnake, as this fear will prompt you to not go near it. This is rational fear. This is your survival instinct kicking in.

However, there are other types of fear that, simply put, are completely irrational and don't really serve a purpose. They are merely based on some sort of programming, false belief system, or past traumatic experience.

Some fears are more subtle and harder to detect - such as the fear of failure, rejection, or loneliness. These are fears that you have to dig a little bit deeper to uncover. However, whether our fears are subtle or obvious, most of them are irrational and we experience them on a REGULAR basis. So if you have some crazy fears, please don't be ashamed of yourself and know that we all have them. Some of us are just better than others at hiding it.

I'm a strong believer that the right questions can help you find the right answers. So I have prepared you some questions to answer to unveil your fears and try to overwhelm them.

The first section is about detecting your major fears. You will need to have your goal or goals in mind and unveil the fear that doesn't allow you to go further and then you have to fill the deep motivation of this fear, you might need a little bit more of time for this column. Then, you need to know if these fears are realistic, you can do that by knowing your feelings when facing the fear.

The second part of the exercise is about winning the fears and what you think about fears now that you achieved your goal.

Face Your Fears

Which fear limits your ability to pursue your goals?

Goal	Fear	deep motivation
....	....	....
....	....	....
....	....	....

For each of your fears, try to see if it's realistic.
Does this fear make sense?
Is it rational?
Is it logical?
Is it true?

Take in mind just one fear and answer at the following questions:

How would you act differently if you were overcome this fear and focus on what matters?

Which thoughts and feelings do you have when faced with this fear?

- ○ ....
- ○ ....
- ○ ....
- ○ ....

~~~~~~~~~~~~~~~~~~~~~~~~~~~~~~

It is time to act!

1 - Make a list of six small things you could do to face it up, from the easiset to the hardest

- ○ ....
- ○ ....
- ○ ....
- ○ ....
- ○ ....
- ○ ....

2 - Achieve these steps!

3 - Once you have achieved them, will it change your ability to manage and look at this fear in the future?

[yes] [no] If yes, how? ....

Chapter 5
Take action and get to know yourself better

True self-confidence comes from knowing and accepting yourself - including any weaknesses and insecurities - on a deep level. But how do you truly know yourself? How do you know what is actually *you*, and what is just a reflection of the expectations people have of you?

Are you really that dull maths teacher that only wears shades of brown and speaks in monotone - or is this the path you fell into to meet expectations, meanwhile suppressing your self-expression in order to fit snugly within the mold where you put yourself? Are you really the perfectly primped party girl you project on Saturday nights or via your social media profiles, or is this a two-dimensional persona you created to feel accepted and popular, while your true passions and goals are suppressed to make way for this full-time facade?

Don't sit back and let this front you put up define you, or not only will the world never see the real you, but neither will you! Just because you think that your passion doesn't fit in with the pre-existing persona, you have built for yourself - for instance, if you're that maths teacher but actually dreams of acting on stage, or the on-fleek party girl whose true passion is to write comic books. You can't live your life as a stereotype, aligning yourself 100% with an existing trope. You can still be that maths teacher or that party girl - but you can combine this side of yourself with acting out your wildest aspirations that may shock the people in your life to learn, then you are on the road to fully knowing and accepting yourself as the full and oftentimes random package that you are.

This decision to act out your goals, no matter what others may think, will not only reveal your potential but will also take you down a journey of self-discovery. You must get the ball rolling and lean towards whatever is pulling you in - or it will only tease you for the rest of your life - plaguing you with a soul-destroying stream of "what if" s.

That first leap into action

Once you have fixed your goals, thanks to the previous chapters, you can now start to take action. Sure, it may seem a bit off-putting at best and terrifying at worst. But after having done whatever you fear a few to a dozen times or so, you may think: *'Is this it? Is this what I kept putting off for so long?"*

You may almost feel disappointed with this apparent anti-climax after such a long and arduous climb to the top. You may even get a little angry with yourself and wonder why you avoided doing it for so long if it was apparently not such a big deal after all. But contrary to what you may be feeling, this was a big deal. The action itself may be small - especially that first step - but the psychological leap it took to get you there was huge. Now that you have opened the tap and felt that first trickle, the rest should come gushing. You are now ready to take action in your new norm.

Self-confidence can diminish over time if you don't hone and sharpen your skills, if you hit setbacks and don't approach them in a healthy way, or if you don't set out to take action on the regular. Even as you become more self-confident and notice positive changes in yourself, you should still continue to practise your skills to maintain and boost your self-confidence even more. You won't wake up one morning and think - "*wow, I made it, I achieved self-confidence.*" It's a never-ending journey, I'm afraid! This is why constant action on your part is essential. It's all well and good to basque in your newfound sense of self-confidence, but that high will wear off pretty quick if you don't make the most of this shiny new mindset and put yourself to work!

You can visualize and practice positive thinking all you want, but until you step up and actually prove to yourself what you're capable of, then your journey to self-confidence is not yet complete. Consider this quote:

"One important key to success is self-confidence. An important key to self-confidence is preparation." — Arthur Ashe

So now that we're on the same page when it comes to taking action, where do you even begin?

Setting Intentions

Setting intentions can vastly improve your self-confidence and dedication to your goals. Intentions are the fuel to your aspirations and the framework of your motivation. In the short-term, setting intentions can help you get a grip on negative thought-spiraling to cultivate a more positive way of thinking. And in the long-term, setting intentions may be that final step you need to take to achieve self-confidence

The most common example of how setting intentions can trigger concrete results is the placebo effect. You may have heard of it: this is when the *belief* that you will experience something causes you to genuinely experience it. In some clinical research studies, sugar pills have the same effect as aspirin simply because the participants *believe* they are getting the pain-killing medication, and so expect that their pain will be numbed. As a result, they really do feel relief from their suffering. Similarly, people can act as though they are intoxicated after drinking non-alcoholic drinks, simply because they believe it to contain alcohol. Maybe you've experienced it yourself – have you ever felt specific side-effects immediately after reading them on the bottle? Or have a go-to remedy that, although you know isn't science-based, due to the positive associations you have with it, seems to cure any ailment anyway? Hey, if it does the job...

As touched upon in the earlier section on "The Law of Attraction," these kinds of instances really make you think how simply imagining or believing something can somehow summon it into existence. In the same way, your expectations of how you will feel after taking aspirin or drinking a cocktail can shape your experience, expectations of how you will perform in an exam or a race can also have a profound impact on the actual result.

Setting intentions also gives you a feeling of inner strength to deal with tough times. As discussed, positive thinking really is transformative for your entire outlook on life. Replacing self-flagellating thoughts with positive affirmations and reminding yourself that your self-worth isn't affected by any failures, setbacks, or negative comments from others - can reduce your anxiety, make you feel more capable, and ultimately, more self-confident. The same goes for taking action with these positive intentions in mind. Don't begin a new venture thinking "it probably won't work out anyway," "I will probably have to give up" only sets this version of events in motion. By rising to a challenge with affirmations such as "this will be a great experience," or "I am really good at this, so I know I can succeed," in mind, your outcome may well look very different.

Change your habits

We already talked about how changing your habits is always tough, since you have essentially biologically wired yourself through repetition to do things a certain way - whether that's what time you get up, lighting a cigarette on your coffee break, or staring at your phone every night before you sleep. But as already touched upon, you can use this niggling nature of habits to your advantage when it comes to adopting new, positive ones.

The promise of a reward is fundamental to successful habit-setting - whether it's something as simple as allowing you to watch an episode of your favorite show after 2 hours of solid work, or as big as planning to go on your dream holiday once you finish writing your thesis. The question you need to ask yourself is: how do you make new habits stick when your nature doesn't seem to be on your side? We went over how repetition is an important factor, but this is but one piece of the puzzle. Experts propose that in order to successfully maintain healthy habits, you simply must anticipate that you will have pitfalls. Without this realist attitude, when it comes to inevitable obstacles and setbacks that will come your way, the slightest cheat or bump in the road may just throw you. However, if you take off down the road expecting it to be bumpy, then you hold on tight, brace yourself, and will maybe even enjoy the ride!

The Habit Loop – how it can be danger and an opportunity

The Habit Loop is the neurological pattern that governs any habit. It consists of three elements: the cue (what triggers your impulse), the routine (how you carry out your habit), and finally, the reward (how you achieve satisfaction at the end). An awareness of these components and how they translate for you, personally, is key to understanding how you can replace any bad habits you may have with good ones.

Since the habit loop has a hold over your automatic responses to the stimuli in your environment, short-circuiting this cycle can be your ticket to overwriting your bad habits once and for all.

Elements of the Habit Loop:

The Cue

This part is whatever triggers your habit. In general, the cue fits into one of the following categories: your current location, the time of day, your company, or whether you're alone, your emotional state, or what you were doing immediately before.

For example, the smell of fresh ground coffee as you walk past the coffee shop each day may make you instinctively reach for your wallet to place an order. Or the nostalgic jingle of fairground music may make you crave junk food you would never normally consume. Alternatively, being around certain friends or in a party setting may make you habitually drink more alcohol than you usually would, or smoke a cigarette. And being bored or lonely may be what triggers your nail-biting. Whatever the specific cue, this is what tells the brain to go into "automatic processing" mode, as your body has learned that the response to this stimuli is to carry out the habit in question. This means that it takes some real effort to resist the satisfaction it promises, as it has essentially become second-nature to you. If you fail to complete the loop once it's started, it physically and mentally pains you. Your brain has been hardwired to expect a particular reward to follow this cue and knows exactly what it must do to get it. And yet you say *no*. Even though denying yourself from this instant pleasure hit makes you feel incomplete until this neurological request is fulfilled.

On top of that, with the plethora of stimuli bombarding you each day, isolating your bad habit's cue in order to overcome it is a challenging feat. But of course, you can do it if you set your mind to it. Try to determine what exactly is triggering your habit by keeping the below questions in mind next time that familiar urge strikes. Notice any patterns that may emerge when you ask yourself:

Where are you right now?

What time of day is it?

What's your emotional state?

Who else is with you?

What were you doing immediately before this urge struck?

The Routine

A habit's routine is the most obvious element: it's the behavior you wish to change. This could smoking, biting your nails, or

Most habits have a pretty easily identifiable routine. This is the repeated behavior that you want to change.

The Reward

It's the memory of a past reward that's the reason why your brain insists on repeating this habit loop in the first place. After a previous fulfillment of the routine, it had been flooded with happy hormones due to you succumbing to the activity provoked by the cue. Your reward provides positive reinforcement for this habit, making it more likely that you will repeat the behavior later on. Your reward could be anything, whether something tangible - like a sugar rush or a nicotine fix, to something more intangible such as the validation you get from checking your Instagram notifications, watching your favorite television series, or playing a video game.

One thing to note is that the reward may not be as obvious as you think. For instance, the reward for your daily craving for a morning latte could be just the caffeine fix; it could just as well be the heightened sense of self-worth you feel subconsciously by going into that trendy coffee shop where the music makes you feel like you're in an art-house film and they know your name and order, or even as simple as the energy boost from the calories in the milk - which you could get just as easily from an apple or banana.

Experimenting with these potential rewards is the time-consuming part of getting a hold over your habits. This means that every time you feel that familiar hard-to-resist urge to repeat your habit loop routine, just try changing it. See what happens. Change the reward to see if it gives you the same satisfaction you crave. Keep track of your mood and craving changes and test different possibilities. And each time you try out an alternative routine after 15 minutes have passed, ask yourself after if you're still craving the original reward. You may just discover that once your true craving for social interaction, a few calories, or simply a break from your computer screen has been met, the original desire dissipates. It doesn't have a hold on you anymore.

Just Keep Going

You will already know that starting a new habit is difficult, so I will spare you the spiel. But when you try to achieve the result you want right away with your maximum level of effort, you tend to only make things harder on yourself and make failure more likely.

For example, if you wish to instill the habit of exercising more regularly, you may well decide to start off by working out for just an hour or two every day. Doesn't seem excessive, right? But after a week or so, you discover that devoting a large amount of time to a whole new fitness regimen when your body or lifestyle is not yet accustomed to it, is too difficult and unrealistic to maintain. Ultimately, you give up. I'm sure that pretty much all of us have experienced a situation like this at some point. You believe yourself to be a failure because you couldn't follow through with your original plan.

But what if I told you that it was actually the plan itself that was truly to blame? As already stressed at length, you must always be realistic when setting goals, despite your impatience to go from 1 to 100 in one unsustainable swoop. If you're truly in this plan for the long-haul, then you can't expect a quick fix or an overnight transformation. Set habits you can realistically stick to in the long-term, and keep going. Little by little. A tiny push every day. You barely even notice the strain, but you improve a little bit with every practice. Then, before you know it, your progress will be more than you could have hoped for.

Habit-setting expert Leo Babauta claimed that '*actually making the habit is much more important than how much you do,*' and I simply must agree. If you want to develop the habit of exercising more, for instance, the most important thing is for you to do the exercise on a regular basis, rather than focusing too much on your performance from the get-go. You could try doing half an hour a day for two weeks - you may not manage to keep going the whole time for the first few days, but as long as you keep showing up and trying your hardest each time, you will gradually find it more manageable. And so, a new habit will form. Before long, you will start to crave the exercise on cue, as your body becomes accustomed to the practice. Big improvements start small!

But what if you just don't want to?

Let's be honest, though - sometimes, you just don't feel it. You know that you *should* be doing something, but finding the motivation to get to it can be an uphill struggle. You may have a difficult task ahead of you that just gives you the childish urge to give up and hide.

It may be the physical slog of getting started, or that the particular task in question is something that makes you particularly uncomfortable - such as a frightening phone call or writing a report you just can't seem to feel invested in. Alternatively, maybe you just had a bad day and have lost interest. We've all been there. It can be uncomfortable, emotionally and physically draining, or just plain boring. We'd much rather be doing something else, and our overworked, understimulated minds can find this terribly frustrating.

And yet, there's no getting past the fact that taking action is the only way to kickstart your ambitions into motion. But how do you push yourself to do this when much of your mind and body just doesn't want to? How do you push yourself to take action, even if you don't feel that motivation kicking in yet?

If you're anything like most of my clients (or most people in general, I'm sure!), then you tend to instinctively use self-criticism as your key motivator. In other words, you instinctively bully yourself into taking this necessary action, as it seems like the only option left. Although this may sometimes work, as there's nothing like a bit of self-loathing to then decide to further punish yourself, it's quite simply not an effective (or desirable) strategy to take. This is because it fails to nourish a healthy relationship to yourself and leads to even more problems with your self-esteem down the line.

Furthermore, research has found a link between self-criticism and "unhealthy, avoidant behavior." Think watching TV till your eyes are sore, playing video games till reality starts to glitch, or binge eating. You know you shouldn't. But why is it so *tempting*? One thing you can take away from this is that beating yourself into submission is not a practical strategy to become productive, as it triggers the natural urge within all of us to resist coercion. This is why it's also the kids with the strictest parents who act up. Our evolutionary history has conditioned us to dig our heels firmly into the ground when we feel we are being pushed against our will - something that can help strengthen your defense against competitors or bullies but also is the reason behind your stubbornness.

But what if your next adversary is actually yourself? When you are your own worst critic, this can give you the perfect excuse to do exactly the opposite of what you are leading with yourself to put your mind to. That lingering infantile and impulse-driven voice inside of you cries, *"I don't want to!"* or *"you can't make me"* - and as you may well be aware, this little voice has a great track record for getting what it wants. It takes a softer approach to see real results.

Below are six steps to help you get over the internal barriers that are stopping you from being the person you truly want to be. It all starts with some acknowledgment and awareness of some hard-to-accept truths...

Step 1: Know When to Stop

Before you can even hope for anything to change, you must acknowledge that sometimes, you just don't feel like taking action. It could be the feelings it evokes - maybe frustration, resentment, boredom - or possibly even depression. It could simply be that you are overworked and sleep or nutrient-deprived. Or it could just be a bad day for you, where you feel incapable of accomplishing anything.

When you are in this state of mind, no matter how much you would *like* to be motivated, you're quite simply, and unavoidably, *not*. There's, unfortunately, no foolproof motivation button to quickly set you in productivity mode.

We are humans - not robots! And sometimes our annoyingly human emotions and unexplained moods take center stage.

Unfortunately, we often cling to our quest for "good" feelings, which can lead to a lot of trouble. When we obsessively pursue these "good" feelings, we tend to avoid any activity that could evoke difficult feelings. It's for this reason that we often avoid and postpone taking action. *(Hello procrastination, my old friend.)*

Consequently, the first step towards making yourself take action like a boss is to quit trying to feel "good" every minute of the day. Not only is this setting you up for disappointment, but it is a silly goal anyway - as without any level of hardship or difficulty, we would not even appreciate the good moments at all. So let go of your idea that you must feel 100% before you begin that task. Although it's important to take breaks, and not lose sight of your physical and emotional boundaries, being too easy on yourself will only make it even harder to take the necessary action.

Step 2: Make Room for your Discomfort

But it's not enough to give up on your attachment to feeling good - you also need to come to a truce with your negative emotions. If not, the battle will never end... As mentioned, taking action can provoke a lot of difficult thoughts and feelings. And as long as you're still grappling with your own feelings of discomfort, you will continue struggling to finally take action.

And so, instead of regarding your negative feelings as the enemy, allow yourself to experience them. Stop trying to push them away or avoid them, and simply let them exist for a while – as they will inevitably exit the same way they came! Until you let these niggling negative emotions pass through you, they will keep on nagging at your consciousness, rattling the door to your mind. By making room for your feelings of discomfort and allowing yourself to feel bored, frustrated, angry, or whatever else, you will finally be able to face the reasons behind these emotions and stop living in fear of them. You will finally be able to experience them in order to manage them, and ultimately, to let them go.

Have you ever kept pushing off a task because it brought you such a sense of dread? But then once you eventually forced yourself to get stuck in, it wasn't nearly as difficult as you'd imagined? Well, this is often the case: it is the anticipation of a difficult task that is the worst part. The doing itself is often a breeze in comparison!

This doesn't mean, of course, that you will actually enjoy these difficult feelings. However, it does mean that your difficult feelings don't need to disappear before you can do what truly matters for you. You can let them in, let them go, and be ready for your next challenge. The sooner you allow yourself to actually feel the discomfort you fear, the faster you can start to take the action required to achieve your goals.

Step 3: Connect With Your Reasoning

That being said, there's no need to feel discomfort if it's not in the name of something necessary and worthwhile. You must keep reminding yourself of what it's all for. The trick is to figure out what truly matters to you, personally, and base your motivation on this. Why is it necessary for *you*, personally, to take action? It could be to enhance your career, improve your health, or realize a lifelong dream.

Meanwhile, try to let go of any reasons behind your motivation that come from compliance, the validation of others, or the avoidance of your own guilt or self-loathing. Instead, focus on taking action for whatever ranks highly for you. Ensure that it's a free choice, as this is the kind of reasoning that really counts. So come to terms with your own goals and values, and let these be what fuels you towards action.

Step 4: Commit to your Commitments

Now comes that oh-so-pivotal moment where you set your commitments. But what are you willing to commit to? It needn't be something huge. You can start with a simple goal, and exercise your willpower over time by gradually pushing your limits - just like you would a muscle. For instance, instead of going for a 5km swim off the bat, start by going for just 500 meters and then gradually increase each time.

Don't forget that you get to call the stops here - so make them count, but also make them realistic. What are you committing to do? When and where exactly are you committing to do it? The more specific and tailored to your own life and routine, the better.

Step 5: Take That First Step

This is the part when you really get down to it and *do something.* Now. No matter how small your first step may be. Once you set your intention in motion in the form of an action, then a big part of the work is already done. Often, it is that gaping blank page - either metaphorical or not - that convinces us that we *can't*, or that we *shouldn't*. However, once you get the ball rolling, you'll be a force to be reckoned with - trust me!

So just dive in and take that first baby step. And then do the next thing and the next… follow through with the commitments you laid out for yourself. But stay with the process. Don't let your inner critic start bossing you around or sabotaging your plans. If you begin to falter, then go back through the four steps above. You got this.

Step 6: Own Your Inaction

When your willpower falters, ask yourself this: *who's commanding you to take action?* It's you that is in charge here. It was your decision to push yourself in this way. Similarly, by also owning your inaction, you are owning your responsibility. Are you unhappy with your results? That's okay - you have no one to answer to, and no one to blame but yourself. There's no obligation here. It's a question of choice: *your choice.*

Once you come to terms with the fact that you're in the front seat of your own life and both your successes and failures are your own, then it can be surprisingly calming. Once you shake off this infantile mindset of "I don't want to," "you can't make me," that you're intrinsically hardwired to resist, then you can accept your own authority. And it's not such a big deal if you do decide to take a break or to change your course. Just do so with the right intentions - because this is what you believe is best for you - not simply to dodge negative feelings such as fear, laziness, or frustration.

You have the ability to choose your own plan of action - when to push forward and when to step back - based on what works best for you overall, whether your inner critic likes it or not! So just as you should own your decisions to take that mighty step forward, you also need to take back ownership over your decision to step back.

Take action: Some Final Thoughts

So there you have my six steps you must take in order to break down those self-imposed barriers holding you back and to start doing what *really* matters to you and aligns with your aspirations - despite the inevitable challenges you must face along the way. It's time to let go of the idea that you must feel good every minute of the day, and allow yourself to experience those unavoidable difficult feelings in order to overcome them.

Reflect on why taking action in your life is important to you, and commit to what exactly you will do in order to ultimately reach your goals. And lastly, when you must pause or take a step back, *own* this intentional inaction. Beating yourself into submission is not an efficient nor an appealing strategy. You shouldn't have to bully yourself in order to care.

Training No. 5
Habit loop

In this chapter, you will hopefully have understood that in order to become more self-confident, you have to start doing something!

You will start to reach your first goals by taking those little steps that will allow you to get out of your comfort zone and, overcoming the first obstacles and fears, and to set your plan in motion. Once you pass this initial phase and get your first results, you will become more and more confident in yourself, finding yourself in a sort of positive habit loop.

This is exactly what you must aim for. Make sure that the steps you have taken to overcome your fears are transformed from a rare exception to a non-stop routine. Routine can be good or bad; it depends on how and to what extent you are trapped.

For example, if you are working on a big project and you need concentration but at one point you receive a notification on your phone, your phone rings, you get distracted and curious by it, you drop your task, losing concentration for your primary focus and start to scroll your Facebook newsfeed. Guess what? This is a bad habit loop!

But then there are good loops, for example, the morning routine, the fact that you need to spend time for yourself.

In this training, we will use the law of habits and routine to our advantage, putting into practice what I have already explained to you about this mechanism. You must think deeply about a habit that you want to transform into an automatic routine. Once you have done this, try to do the exercise and practice it every day.

Habit loop

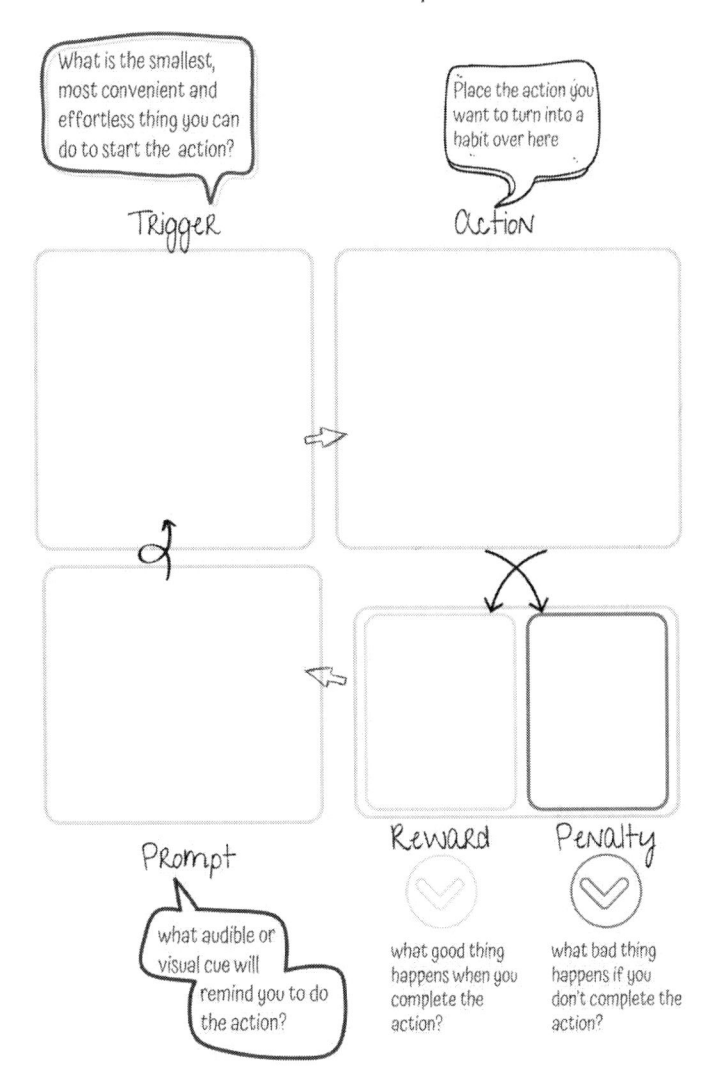

Trigger

What is the smallest, most convenient and effortless thing you can do to start the action?

Action

Place the action you want to turn into a habit over here

Prompt

what audible or visual cue will remind you to do the action?

Reward

what good thing happens when you complete the action?

Penalty

what bad thing happens if you don't complete the action?

Chapter 6

You've got to experience failure to understand that you can survive it

We have talked about owning your inactivity and not being afraid of setbacks or bumps in the road, but it can still often prove difficult to use the F word... by which I, of course, mean *failure*.

When you hear the world "failure," it may leave you with connotations of despair, humiliation, or a complete dead end. But your failures needn't feel like this! Failing in one particular route simply teaches you something - either about yourself or about the project you attempted. Is this the right project for you? If so, how could you have done it differently to achieve the desired result?

The issue is that since our earliest experiences in formal education, we have been trained to focus on getting things right first time, and to avoid making mistakes at all costs. A mistake meant an unappealing red cross - or worse still, that obnoxious "F" scrawled across your page. And so, our fear of getting it wrong starts at a very early age. We set ourselves up for a turbulent relationship with our failures before we even go through puberty.

I propose that rather than seeing failure as a dead-end, regard it like a slight bump in the road that causes you to change course. You may slightly veer off the original path you set out for yourself when confronted with a failure, but it needn't be a complete U-turn. Before you completely abandon the mission, simply re-evaluate your route, and find an alternative way to get to your desired destination.

Still not convinced? Here are the positives you can think of the next time you fail, broken down:

Analyzing Failure

Once you experience failure and want to figure out why it happened, go beyond the more obvious or superficial reasons, and to delve deeper to understand the root cause. This requires both objectivity and enthusiasm in order to ensure that the appropriate lessons are learned and that the suitable remedies are administered.

Why do we often get this analysis part wrong? Well, I'd say it's because examining our failures in depth when all we really want to do is bury them and never look back, is quite simply rather unpleasant emotionally, and can threaten that self-confidence we tried so hard to build up. Without adequate self-discipline and the motivation to learn from what happened, most of us will choose to avoid failure analysis altogether - maybe even deeming it the productive or confidence-preserving thing to do. Sure, it may seem like forgetting these lower moments is better for our newly fragile ego, but the longer we put off this necessary processing step, the more painful it will become when we inevitably must face up to it in the future. This is why these past failures tend to creep up on you as you try to fall asleep and let your mental guard start to slip. They have not been sufficiently processed, and so they will continue to haunt you until you can close the door on them.

And the struggle to move on from our failures is more than just emotional: it's cognitive, too. This is because we subconsciously tend to favour evidence that supports our existing beliefs instead of any alternative explanation. Another ego-preserving move we are also often guilty of when we fail is our underestimation of our own responsibility over the outcome, instead placing undue blame on external or situational factors. Worse still - we then do the opposite when assessing the failures of others—deeming them more responsible than they perhaps are. This psychological trap known as *fundamental attribution error* is prime evidence of how our flimsy, suggestible perspectives often can't be trusted at face value - and so, an objective analysis is key.

Types of Failure

Another thing to note is that not all failures were created equal. Developing an understanding of each failure's many potential causes and contexts will help you to avoid this twisted blame game, and instead implement a trusted and effective strategy to truly learn from every mistake in a constructive yet not a self-punishing way.

Our failures fall into these three overarching categories:

Preventable failures (Independent)

Failures falling under this category usually involve either an accidental or experimental deviation from the rules. For example, trying a new ingredient in your tried-and-tested cake batter that didn't turn out quite right. Or, a technical hitch in your coding due to your own human error. In this scenario, you know exactly where you went wrong. This is why I call them "preventable." Despite how it may look, I don't use this word simply to rub your nose in it that you allowed it to happen! But rather, these failures are defined by a relatively simple and easily identifiable error. Many of these "errors" were either intended as a form of experimentation, due to external factors or down to your state of wellbeing at the time (maybe you were tired or ill, which made you less sharp) - so don't beat yourself up about it! And although this makes it all the more annoying, it also makes it much easier to learn from, as you know exactly what to change for future attempts.

Unavoidable Failures (Blameless)

Then there are plenty of failures where what went wrong is much more tricky to pinpoint. They may be due to the inherent uncertainty behind the work – for instance, if you fail on a big project, you weren't well prepared for, and there were countless things you could have improved on along the way. It could also be a failure due to a very specific and unpredictable combination of requirements, obstacles, or setbacks that came along the way. Think the teams of doctors in an accident and emergency department – they may not always save the patient – but this was most likely not their fault. Maybe the patient had undiagnosed complications, maybe the doctor didn't have the adequate supplies on time, or maybe the patient was simply untreatable. This is a failure, no doubt – but the issue had so many complexities and moving parts that the blame cannot be easily allocated. At least not at first. The same goes for failures on the battlefield of a warzone, or even keeping your new business afloat. What do all these scenarios have in common? Unpredictable situations you were not or *could not* be prepared for, and the dependence on many external outcomes.

Intelligent Failures (Trial and Error)

Failures in this category are the most likely to provide you with valuable new knowledge and potential for personal growth—which is why a professor of management at Duke University, Sim Sitkin, named them "intelligent failures." They occur when experimentation is required, and failures are to be expected. The pharmaceutical company, Eli Lilly, has held "failure parties" since the early 1990s in order to celebrate those many scientific experiments that - although intelligent by design, and well-prepared - simply fail to achieve the desired results. Although perhaps taken to the extreme here (each to their own!) it is perhaps a more widely accepted fact among the scientific community that failure needn't always be such a bad thing if you see it as a necessary and well-intentioned step closer to the successful outcome you crave. After all, countless experiments need to be carried out to make new discoveries - and not all of them will be as fruitful as hoped. But that's just part and parcel of the long game. Trial and error. Learning from past results and moving forward.

All in all, we can actually learn a lot from this scientific approach to failure in the last category and apply it to our mistakes that are far removed from the lab. Why not treat your future failed endeavors as though they were science experiments? Sure, it may not have quite hit the mark this time - but this is all a part of the process!

Why we are so Fearful of Failure

Our partially intrinsic and partially ingrained tendency to hope for the best and avoid failure at all costs can get in the way of our progress and ambition. The remedy is - quite simply - to reduce the stigma of failure. But this is easier said than done.

Have you ever felt so frightened of failing, that you ultimately decided not to try at all? Has a fear of failure caused you to belittle your own abilities to avoid the possibility of humiliation? "I'm *not good anyway.*"… "*That dream would never go anywhere.*"… sound familiar? Just imagine all of the initiatives you may have attempted if this stomach-lurching fear of failure and humiliation wasn't there to rein you back in? Sure, you may have failed some or even most of these endeavors. But what if just one of these supposedly crazy ideas turned out to be a huge success? All it takes is one positive outcome, after all - so it pays to have probability in your favor.

Many of us have probably experienced this self-sabotaging fear at one time or another. The fear of failure can be debilitating - it can cause us to be apathetic, and even cynical, as we relentlessly convince ourselves that we shouldn't take the risk. You may be afraid of failing, simply because you desire to do well. This is, for the most part, manageable - as long as you keep your self-confidence in check and are able to learn and move on from these mistakes, as discussed. However, if you really struggle to shake off your fear of failure - called "atychiphobia" in its chronic form - this runs the risk of preventing you from progressing as you hope and stands in the way of you achieving your goals.

A chronic fear of failure can be due to various factors. For instance, having critical or unsupportive parents, guardians, or teachers while growing up (look back at the first chapter's section on self-acceptance for more information on how this can affect you psychologically in the long term). A specific traumatic event from your adulthood can also be a cause: For instance, if you once gave an important presentation to a large group of people and it went very badly. It could have been any past failure that you found so humiliating or emotionally scarring that you became irrationally afraid of failing in other things as a defense mechanism to avoid these feelings in the future.

So do you have a healthy determination to succeed, or a chronic phobia of failure?

Well, do any of these signs pointing at the latter sound familiar?

A reluctance to try new things or and a lack of motivation when presented with a new task or project.

Self-sabotaging behaviour such as procrastination, excessive anxiety, or a tendency to bail on your own goals before they're complete.

Low self-confidence reflected by frequent use of negative statements along the lines of *"I'll never be good enough"* or *"what's the point in even trying?"*

Perfectionism to the point that it becomes an addictive behavior. You limit yourself to tasks that you know you'll finish with relative ease to avoid potential failure.

How Not to Be Afraid of Failure

Whether you're a part-time panicker or a full-time failure-phobe, we must all learn to accept and live with the fact that whatever we do, there is always the chance that we'll fail. Unappealing as this thought may seem, the more familiar we are with it, the less hard we will take any future failures. You will realize that failure is an inevitability, and should not be a blow to your ego or received as a sign that you should give up. Facing up to the possibility of failure and plowing on with your ideas regardless is not only a courageous and confidence-boosting move, but it basically promises a more fulfilling and satisfying life.

To summarise a few ways to reduce your fear of failure:

Analyze all potential outcomes to bust that fear of the unknown. This way - you will have already come to terms with all possible failures - including the absolute worst-case scenario - before any of them even have a chance to happen. It takes away that element of heart-sinking surprise and means you dive in with your eyes wide open.

As discussed at great length in Chapter 3, train yourself to think more positively and banish your negative inner monologue. Positive thinking is an unassumingly effective way to build your self-confidence, improve your overall outlook on life, and neutralize any self-sabotaging thoughts.

Always have a Plan B in mind. If you feel afraid of failing something, having this "Plan B" already thought out can help you to be confident in the strides you take.

You could also keep in mind an inspirational quote about success or failure and use it like a mantra. Remember it whenever a failure risks derailing your self-confidence. Here are a few of my favorites:

"Our greatest glory is not in never falling but in rising every time we fall." - Confucius

"Behind every successful man, there are a lot of unsuccessful years." - Bob Brown

"Only those who dare to fail greatly can ever achieve greatly." - Robert F. Kennedy

Learning through "Safe" Failure

According to Learning Solutions Magazine, learning through "safe" failure is essential for personal growth. The key to this is evaluating each failure you make, and ranking the consequences rationally according to their severity. It may seem like the end of the world at the moment that that job you were pining for fell through, but how much is this going to seriously impact you in the long run? Try ranking each setback from a scale of insignificant impact, moderate impact, significant impact, and finally – critical impact.

For instance, that one job application or publication submission rejection is most likely only going to inflict an insignificant impact upon your life, in the wider scheme of things. A noticeable but not life-changing financial loss may be ranked at "moderate" or "significant." But your business is collapsing, or your marriage failing may well be scored as critical.

Most likely, you will find, your failures will be in the mildest two categories. However, we all face failures with critical consequences at some point in our lives. No words I can write to you will help you to overcome these, so I won't attempt to do that. However, what I *can* offer you is reassurance that even the failures at this most unfortunate end of the spectrum can be overcome. Even when you feel like you're in the depths of despair and there seems to be no hope, if you manage to build your self-confidence enough to establish a healthy level of stable self-esteem, then come what may, you will have more emotional strength to face the inevitable failures along your personal path towards success.

The Importance of Resilience

Psychologists define resilience as our process of adapting and remaining strong in the face of significant sources of stress or trauma - such as failure. Resilience may imply our ability to brush ourselves off and bounce back from these difficult experiences and into the next challenge, as well as the profound possibility for personal growth and self-discovery.

This is because improving your emotional resilience not only helps you to survive and thrive through life's more difficult circumstances, but it will also empower you to improve your life, and grow along the way.

What Resilience Doesn't Mean

Of course, being resilient doesn't mean that a person simply will not experience difficulty or distress. As touched upon, these negative feelings are often unavoidable - and it is actually more constructive to expect and embrace such feelings to ultimately be able to recover from them and move on.

And while there are personality traits that may make some people more resilient than others, resilience isn't necessarily a personality trait in itself. Perhaps, fortunately, for most, resilience involves behaviors, thought processes, and actions that anyone is able to learn and develop.

Just like building up a muscle, increasing your level of resilience requires patience, effort, and determination. You can do this by focusing on four main components — relationships, emotional wellness, healthy mindset, and maintaining a purpose. If you hold onto these four simple areas of your life and value them sufficiently, they can empower you to withstand the tough times and learn from difficult experiences such as failure.

Connecting with others

Firstly, in terms of relationships, connecting with the understanding people in our lives - whether our friends, family, or partner - reminds us that we're not alone when our mistakes and failures threaten to tarnish our sense of self-worth and self-confidence. The pain of facing the disappointment of failure can tempt us to isolate ourselves to avoid the threat of others' judgment, but it's important to accept help and support from those who care about us. Whether you have a daily with a family member or a weekly lunch with your close friend, you must prioritize cultivating these genuine connections with the people in your life who care about you.

Emotional wellness

Don't forget to take adequate care of your body, as well as your mind, as a priority. Self-care may be a buzzword of our times, but this umbrella term encapsulates whatever personal rituals make you feel both comforted and alive. Self-care is also a crucial practice for mental health and a key component to building sufficient resilience. This is because stress is both a physical and an emotional threat - both in terms of causes and consequences. Promoting positive lifestyle factors such as ample nutrition, sleep, hydration, and exercise can strengthen both your body and your mind - due to your mental health's intimate connection with your physical health. So never push your health to the side, even during testing times! If anything, these are the times where taking care of your body and emotions are even more crucial in order to maintain that magical resilience.

Mindfulness

Being more 'mindful' is another internet buzzword that you may be tempted to brush off as pseudoscience. But mindfulness essentially means being more present - not forever having our consciousness oriented towards the future - whether that's what to cook for dinner tonight, what you're going to respond to that awkward email tomorrow, or where your career will take you five years down the road.

Although, as discussed, planning is important - both for the small stuff and the big - we also must learn how to effectively separate ourselves from this constant habit of thinking ahead to the point that we never truly experience the present. It's a tall task today's reality of smartphones meaning we are constantly plugged into a relentless global conversation, but there are various activities you can incorporate into your daily or weekly routine in order to gradually ground yourself and feel yourself again. For instance, you could try journaling, yoga, or meditation. Not only do these activities bring you some much-needed quiet, and break up your day-to-day rush, but they encourage you to remember that you are alive. Your body and mind are constantly working overdrive just to keep you functioning throughout the day. And so, you should repay them the favor - they will thank you for it!

Seek purpose

Many of us feel a sense of greater purpose when we help others. Whether this means volunteering at a homeless shelter or supporting a friend in a time of need, this enables you to develop a sense of purpose, self-worth, and all while helping others. This is a fine recipe to build your resilience and baseline self-esteem while you're at it.

Be proactive

As discussed, we must acknowledge and accept our emotions during tough and challenging moments, but it's also important during times of hardship to ask ourselves: "What can I do to make things better?" If the problems seem too overwhelming to tackle in one go, there's no shame in breaking them down into manageable pieces. Come up with a small thing you could do right away to even only slightly lighten tomorrow's load. And if you make this small effort every day for a week? A moth? Then, where will you be?

For instance, upon losing your job, you may not be able to just get it back - no matter how determined or resilient you are. However, what you can do each day is spending an hour each day developing your CV and then applying to one or two positions each day. Just this small daily commitment paves the way for huge future benefits. Taking the initiative in this way despite the unfortunate cards you've been dealt with will remind you that you can muster up some motivation and determination - even during stressful or unexpected periods of your life. This only increases your resilience to make you even more confident to rise to challenges and overcome failures in the future.

Take the opportunity for self-discovery

We often find that we grow and improve in some way as a result of a past struggle. For example, after losing a job, ending a relationship, or failing an important exam, many of us go through a dark period. We question who we really are, what we really want, and where our lives are going. This may be a painful process, but we come out the other end with a better knowledge of ourselves. We not only have evidence that we can overcome something truly difficult, but we are forced to really look at ourselves and ask ourselves some deep questions. This is all a part of self-discovery, and should not be underestimated as a great resilience-booster - even if you may not enjoy the process! In the long term, it can actually cause your self-confidence to increase, and your overall self-awareness and self-acceptance will also benefit as a result.

Embrace healthier thoughts

Remember to maintain a rational perspective. Your thought processes are key to shaping your emotions and resilience. As such, attempt to identify bouts of irrational thinking - such as a tendency to catastrophize difficulties or assume the world is out to get you because something didn't go your way - and instead shift into a more balanced and realistic outlook. When feeling overwhelmed by a challenge, remind yourself that whatever happened in the past isn't necessarily an indicator of your future. You may not be able to significantly change a stressful event, but what you *can* change is how you react to it.

Accept change

Learn to accept that changes and unexpected outcomes are a part of life. Certain goals or ideals may have to be changed – not eliminated, but replaced. Sometimes, life gets in the way of our goals, and external factors throw us off course. However, accepting when circumstances cannot be changed will allow more time and energy for you to focus on what you can take control of.

Failure: Some Final Thoughts

All being considered, you may well be thinking – *sure, big up failure all you want – it is still not something anyone strives for or wants for themselves.* And granted, it's not something that you get congratulated for, or go out to celebrate (unless you work for Eli Lilly, of course...) It's a simple fact that, for the most part, failure will lead you down a road of disappointment and grief for what could have been.

However, what we should remember above all else is that we cannot go our whole life without failure – unless, of course, you don't ever try anything at all. And in this case, you have essentially failed yourself. This is where resilience comes in - something you can work on within yourself as a sort of insurance blanket, or emotional cushion, to make any future failures that bit easier to handle.

When a door closes, not only does another door (eventually) open, but you also learn that this initial door was not yours to begin with. So why cry and moan that it has closed, when you could instead by using the time and energy to find your *actual* door?

Many of us are afraid of failing, but we mustn't let that fear become powerful enough to stop us from seizing opportunities, pursuing excitement, or hoping for more. Don't let the failure win - simply let it fuel your inner fire and drive you. In all seriousness, an irrational fear of failure can have several causes - from childhood insecurities to negative experiences during our adult lives. But regardless of the origins of our fears, it's important to realise that we always have a choice of how we respond emotionally to any external factor - which includes, of course, our failures. Often, we get upset simply because we subconsciously deem it the appropriate response - like little kids who don't cry when they first fall, as it didn't really hurt so much, but then start to well up as a reaction to the flapping adults around them. If you develop an awareness of what you really want and how you really feel, separate from the gaze of others, you can get more of a handle on your emotions and become able to keep going no matter what hiccups come along the way.

Furthermore, don't lose sight of the fact that when someone rejects you and you feel your heart start to sink, you are most likely taking their subjective opinion of you as a reflection of your entire value. Surely, this can't be right! And yet we all do it. We take that one "*no*" or *"I don't like it"* as an earth-shattering catastrophe and indisputable confirmation that we suck. Basically, we take their personal opinion of this one fragment of our abilities, and then base our whole self-worth off of it… Not only is this valuing yourself on others' opinions, but their opinions on just one tiny portion of what you actually have to offer.

Doesn't that sound ridiculous when you put it like that? Well, the core issue here is that your self-confidence isn't self generated by you as it ought to be, but is instead defined by external validation. If that is the case, then his isn't real self-confidence at all - but merely a transient sense of satisfaction based entirely on others' praise. Is this what you really want your self-esteem to be based on? Wouldn't you rather be the one in control of your own sense of self?

In the modern world of excessive materialism, performance tracking, and social media boasting, we are desperate for the reminder that failure is not the exception - it's the rule. Failure is a universal experience, but since most people aren't ready to be so loud and proud about these particular moments, we are led to believe that when we fail, there is something wrong with us. Whether that's a work-related blunder, a relationship failure, a parenting mistake, or a misjudgment in your creative endeavors - no matter what you newsfeed may suggest, *you are not alone.* You need to take advantage of what our failures can teach us, and start to see our mistakes as mere guides to lead us onto the correct path - to be acknowledged but not to be mourned!

Have the humility to admit to your mistakes, accept and own them, and then make sure that you make them count in your future projects. Build your emotional resistance with every challenge you face, and let failure be a key motivator, and not only will your fears diminish, but your self-confidence and overall success will soar.

Training No. 6

Emotional resilience and learning from our mistakes

Thanks to this next exercise, you will learn to improve your ability to self-analyse, to recognise what were the mistakes that led you not fulfilling your goals, all with the intention of learning from your mistakes - which, remember, are your most excellent teachers!

Think about five difficult situations where you weren't able to achieve your goal, and for each one of them, answer the following questions.

Emotional resilience and learning from our mistakes

1. What was your goal?
Be specific; you must know what your plan was, otherwise, the first mistake you made could be the wrong goal setting.

2. What was your strategy? How did you act?
Be specific; you must know what your plan was, otherwise, the first mistake you made could be the wrong goal setting.

3. In your opinion, why you haven't achieved your goal?
Please don't blame others, try to analyse everything objectively.

4. What have you learned that will help you do better next time?
If you made a mistake, it means that fortunately, there is something to learn from it, and next time, you won't make the same mistake again.

5. What's the new plan?
Probably you need to fix something, or maybe you should try it again, and this time will definitely be better!

Stop! Stop! Stop!

Here I am again to interrupt your reading!

I just wanted to check how the book was going, but if you got this far, I would say not so bad!

Would you like to let me know your thoughts by leaving a short review on Amazon?

It shouldn't take you too much of your time, but I assure you it would be an invaluable gift for a small writer like me.

I thank you in advance!

Scan me for leaving a review!

Chapter 7
Believe you can and you're already halfway there

So you've really been taken around the houses these last six chapters - from what self-confidence and its counterparts even mean, to how it is required to set goals, take action, and learn from your failures and to build resilience. But now, at risk of sounding like a cheesy 90's mouse mat, all I have left to say to you is this:

Once you truly believe in yourself, you're already halfway there.

It really is true - as I expressed at length in the chapter on the power of positive thinking and the "law of attraction," - if you take away one lasting message from this book, that should be it. Once you tell yourself that you can do something - or better still, that you *will* do something - the odds that it will happen suddenly soar - because that genuine intention is there. And by intention, I don't mean that throwaway "*one day, I'll do that*," though without any commitment or the solid strategy behind it - as these are just as flimsy as they sound.

True intention can be felt within. You may not even voice it out loud, but you know that you will follow through with it, whatever it takes. Once you can visualize a clear idea of what you want to accomplish and the reasons behind it, you can begin comparing each and every task and turmoil against these overall goals and core values. And if your current activity isn't aligned with your overall purpose, then you are only needlessly depleting your energy and passion. Hey - it's better that you realize sooner rather than later!

In this final chapter, let's aim to tie the ends together of the previous pieces of advice offered earlier in the book, and complete it with a rejuvenated sense of positivity and heightened self-awareness - while grounded in the stabilizing force of realism to keep your dreams burning bright - but in a sustainable and controlled way.

Your current mindset is a result of your past

From birth, our brains are still not fully developed. This means that we're born ready and waiting to collect information from our environment and then form beliefs based on this. We then form vital neural connections that then go on to guide us via our thought processes for the rest of our lives. It's kind of amazing but also unnerving, isn't it? That so much goes on in our character development in our first year that we cannot even remember.

The beliefs we form during our childhood and early teenage years form our core beliefs right into adulthood. The experiences during these years are our most influential personality-shapers.

As already discussed right back in Chapter 1, an abused, belittled, or neglected child will form the false belief that they have less value than others because of these formative experiences. They are more likely to become an underconfident, shy, or pessimistic adult as a result of these early experiences, struggling to cultivate a strong sense of self-worth and self-belief.

For instance, a girl whose father abandoned her at a young age may form a belief that men are both some sort of hard-to-reach holy grail, but also fleeting, and untrustworthy. Therefore, she might crave male attention from adolescence but then find it very hard to trust or form an attachment to one particular guy. She might end up sabotaging every relationship to subconsciously avoid getting in too deep to only be let down, or craving the attention and approval of older, paternal men to replace this father-like energy she craved earlier on in life. Either way, this is harmful and worryingly common.

Similarly, a boy who grew up in a family where his parents always worried about money may develop financial insecurity and a strong urge to become rich. He may become very ambitious and competitive - not such a bad thing - but then suffer from depression and anxiety when these constantly increasing goals and increasingly unrealistic expectations are not met. He may remain insecure for the rest of his life about money and not having enough, to the point that he never reaches contentment or fulfillment - even if he gets to a very good place financially. This is because so often, our fears aren't based on our present circumstances, but rather, our past.

Birth order counts

But even the more mundane childhood conditions such as birth order can also have a dramatic effect on how we view ourselves and seek reassurance as adults - so none of us are exempt.

For example, the oldest child in the family may have a lot of expectations pinned on them. They will be the first child of the family to reach each milestone, and may even help out with tending to younger siblings. Meanwhile, the youngest child in a family often is allowed a little more flexibility in terms of behavior, life choices, and often showcases a delayed maturity and sense of responsibility. Most of the projecting and pressure from parents are used up on the first child. Also, without a younger sibling to set an example for, the youngest child is usually more fun-loving and laid back then the eldest.

And so, as adults, the oldest child will likely become more of a headstrong yet sensible go-getter - always striving for the next hurdle and facing challenges head-on. This could be so, whether or not they are self-confident. Like the financially insecure guy discussed earlier, this ambition could be based on fear making it prone to crumbling. Or, this intrinsic determination could be supported by a healthy dose of self-confidence, which can be a killer combination for a successful adult to have. Meanwhile, the youngest child may grow up to be self-confident but in a different way - seeking positive experiences above all else, living in the moment, and with a more relaxed approach to life and how they achieve fulfillment. They may not have the same self-discipline as their older sibling when they grow up (thought this, of course, can be worked upon!), but the youngest child will often be a lot better at taking risks, thinking outside the box, and living in the moment.

If there is a middle child, this is the one likely to have missed out somewhat on the attention. They were not the first, not the last child, so forgo either privilege. They often fill the family role of mediator, adapting to play both with their older and younger siblings, themselves playing both the role of older and younger siblings simultaneously, and becoming a better communicator and empathizer as a result. On the downside, these are the children that often struggle to find their identity or reach self-acceptance as adults, as they spend their childhoods adapting and filling in the gaps, yet not really knowing their own place. A middle child consequently tends to thrive on meaningful relationships and making a positive difference to the lives of others, as this has essentially become their identity - something you should perhaps bear in mind if you are in this position and not sure how to achieve better life-satisfaction!

And then there are the only children, who are stereotypically the loudest and confident people - and for a good reason. Although there will no doubt be exceptions, as there are other factors too, only children from two-parent homes are often on the receiving end of the undivided attention. They grow up under the belief that they are special, unique, and with complete liberty to become whoever they wish, without siblings challenging their requests, or having to share their belongings. All of these factors - both the more subtle and the obvious differences - add up to create that "only child trope" we know so well today. But of course, although many only children grow up to be confident in that they believe in their own abilities and potential, this doesn't mean that they also develop self-efficacy or self-awareness any better than the rest of us. If anything, these two factors may suffer due to the often-stunted communication and self-discipline skills that only children cultivate. So they still have a lot to learn, just like anyone else!

Let your experiences shape and strengthen your character

Overall, we all develop certain personality traits and insecurities as a result of what went on around us as kids, from the unavoidable details about our place within the family, to experiences of trauma or feelings of abandonment. And developing an awareness of how your particular childhood made you who you are today - both the good and the less desirable - is a pivotal point in the road to self-awareness and self-acceptance.

Let this awareness of how our past has carved out our present beliefs and personality be a humbling reminder that even today, our characters are shaped around the experiences we have. Granted, this is not to such an extent as in our formative years while our brains are still wiring themselves up for the first time, but we are never immune to change and adaptation - at any age. And this should be welcome news if you are seeking self-development.

Contrary to popular belief, we can, to a certain extent, still mold our own personalities even during adulthood -

provided we reach a point of self-awareness that most of us struggle to achieve without copious self-reflection and objective study of your past and present fears and desires.

So how do we go about changing our current mindset and beliefs if they become counterproductive or harmful? For instance, the belief that you are not capable or a negative mindset about your future? The first step is to become conscious of where these beliefs may have come from. Negative experiences of the past, or belittling influences in your life that have overwritten your own inner voice. Once you think you've identified the source, then you must reflect on how they may be invalid. They could be the subjective opinions of others, or a one-off event - neither of which should overshadow the beliefs you have in yourself and your life when approached in a rational way.

The forming of beliefs is an unconscious process that may explain why we feel we lack control over it. But once we take proper notice of this process and how it happens, we can grasp a degree of conscious authority over it. This is where the power lies.

Snapping Out of the Victim Mentality

Although we should be aware that our past experiences can profoundly shape who we are today, you should take caution not to slip into a self-sabotaging mindset of victimhood. The truth is that every single person has experienced a level of difficulty and hardship - both in the past and the present. Seeing yourself as a victim as a result of your personal difficulties does not necessarily mean that you have suffered from greater abuse. On a basic level, someone with a victim mentality believes that something or someone has control over what happens in their life - but of course, with an emphasis on the negative. Victims see themselves as somehow lacking in control over their own outcomes. You may - consciously or not - believe life to be against you, or that everyone else somehow has an advantage over you when you see them achieve great things.

The source of this is - once again - low self-confidence. The victim mentality is based on the belief that you are less worthy, and that any disappointment in life stems from this innate victimhood. A lack of respect and good fortune that you feel you receive. You may feel compelled to do things against your will - albeit reluctantly. You may tend to complain a lot to (or about!) those around you, as well as internally. However, you will still find yourself continuing with whatever is causing you so much anguish, falsely thinking that there is no alternative. That you have no choice in the matter other than expressing your disdain. It seems like the whole world is against you because you live passively and unhappily in this way. This is because victims always feel dependent on external forces and blame them for everything that happens. They are the ones who are always asking *"why me?"*

Even in everyday life and through trivial examples, individuals with low self-confidence may succumb to this mentality. For instance, if someone asks you a favor - to get them a cup of tea or to pick up something from the printer for them. You have your own tasks to do and don't want to oblige, and you would never feel self-assured enough to ask even a small favor like this from them. *"The audacity!"* - You scream, silently, as you jump up to fulfill their request...

And so, in this way, you internalize a great deal of anger that you *shouldn't have to* do this. That you are being taken advantage of. And yet, your lack of self-confidence prevents you from actually being assertive enough to voice these thoughts, and so you simply keep your head down and complain to someone else. Meaning that the (often, well-intentioned) asker will do so again, not thinking that you mind at all.

Everybody is tested in this way. At some point, we are all asked or expected to do things we don't feel we should have to do. The difference is that those of us with a healthy level of self-confidence will feel empowered to stand up for ourselves. We may carry out the favor, but also ask similar favors of others to show that this is a give-and-take dynamic. Or, you could politely decline: say "*sorry, I'm super busy right now, can you ask someone else?*" or "*sorry but that's not really my job,*" or whatever the particular circumstances call for.

The point is that you will read the situation and decide what you really ought to be doing, how you can be polite and kind - but not at the expense of your own dignity or wellbeing. Maybe, in reality, you *do* enjoy carrying out favors for others as it gives you a sense of purpose and ultimately is something tangible you can complain about. Or maybe it really *is* a part of your job or allocated responsibility. In which case, any internalized anger and sense of victimhood is a result of feeling undervalued or unfulfilled in yourself. Either way, something needs to be fixed.

The same stands for life's bigger situations. We are often tempted to slip into a victim mentality when things don't go our way. For instance, wallowing in the various reasons beyond your control as the sources of all your problems. "*She wouldn't go out with me because of my height*," or "*I didn't get picked for the promotion because no one really gets me in the office.*" It can be easier on us, psychologically, to pin the blame of our disappointments on something tangible. Rather than looking at ourselves as the complex, flawed individuals that we are, we point the finger and announce a specific cause for our misfortune. This helps us to shift the responsibility of our setbacks - to berate something else, other than ourselves.

In addition to this, for many, the victim mentality can be oddly comforting. On a subliminal level, it makes us feel special and worthy of attention. Individuals struggling with this may crave the acknowledgment of their suffering from others. Because your suffering *is* real - it is simply misunderstood - even by yourself.

If this all sounds worryingly familiar, now that you have identified this obstacle to your self-belief, you can work on fixing it. To overcome your victim mentality, you have to release the negative feelings plaguing your outlook on life: fear, guilt, self-loathing, anger, self-pity. Stop pushing them away. These are the suppressed emotions that keep you enchained to this victim identity. Forgive those who have hurt you - including yourself. Reclaim the power and responsibility in your life by recognizing your own capacity to make changes. And work on changing your inner monologue as well as the vocabulary you use when speaking to others. For instance, instead of "*I can't,*" say "*I will try.*" Instead of complaining about what others have supposedly done to you to cause your present problems, focus on what you are doing now to fix them. Overall, remember that you always have a choice, and that you are no more affected by negative factors than anyone else.

Identify what needs to be fixed

So bearing in mind that your past has carved out your present – but that this goes for all of us, and doesn't make you unique – I cannot stress your need to identify your own problem areas enough. Try to see it this way: let's say your boss at work expressed disappointment at your poor performance last month. She wants you to show evidence of a marked improvement this month. However, she doesn't actually let you know why exactly she believes you underperformed, and what needs to be worked on.

Can you fix anything if you don't know what actually needs to be fixed? Of course not – you need to know precisely what went wrong in order to fix it. Did your absent father cause your abandonment insecurities? Did the fact you were the eldest child give you an impossibly high sense of responsibility and an unquenchable drive to impress? Do you suffer from a victim mentality, making you regard yourself as somehow cheated in life, and doomed to fail?

It's time to face up to the truth of your situation. It may be difficult to accept your flaws in such an objective way, but it will really help you to see yourself more clearly. Don't feel bad or embarrassed - we all have particular complexes that hold us back. But the strength and emotional maturity lie in identifying and overcoming them. In addition to that, you need to know *how* and *why* things go wrong. And the same goes for human psychology on a basic level. Unless you don't understand the underlying meaning or potential issues with your mindset or behavior, you won't know how to change them for the better.

Build your willpower

A growing body of psychological research indicates that willpower and self-discipline are essential for content and fulfilled life. Whatever cards you've been dealt in life - we can all improve our self-discipline and willpower to improve ourselves. To delve a little deeper into this crucial element of self-care (because sometimes, like a parent to a child, we must say "no" for our wellbeing and protection…), I have selected two examples:

The "marshmallow experiment," began in the 1960s by psychologist Walter Mischel. He offered 4-year-olds the opportunity of a marshmallow now, or two if they could wait to receive them in 15 minutes. He and his team then tracked the performance of these children as they grew up. They found that children who had initially resisted temptation for the bigger reward achieved greater academic success, enjoyed better physical health, and generally had lower rates of divorce. Mischel concluded that it was this ability to delay gratification despite temptation constituted '*a protective buffer against the development of all kinds of vulnerabilities later in life.*'

In another study, 1000 children were tracked from birth right up until the age of 32. And again, the results suggested that childhood self-control went as far as to predict physical health, substance dependence, personal finances, and criminal offenses. This was true even when other factors such as personal intellect and social background were factored in. They even found that between siblings living in the same household with the same nature and nurture, the sibling with a lower level of self-control had poorer outcomes later in life, despite the identical family background and upbringing.

Overall, it is clear that the ability to resist instant gratification for a greater and yet longer-term promise of pleasure is key to our success. You can see examples of this wherever you look. From those who choose the instant pleasure of junk food in front of the television over the long-term commitment of taking care of your body - It tends to be the healthy-eater, who sacrifices certain pleasures, which achieves more long-term satisfaction with themselves over the person who succumbs to their every impulse. The same goes for the students who avoid homework for the short-term enjoyment of playing video games - they may have more fun on school nights then their studious counterparts who instead pour over their textbooks, but if the studious ones go one to get good grades and pursue successful career whereas the gamer kid fails and is stuck in an unfulfilling job, then you can see another prime example of how self-discipline really does pay off.

And the same goes for you right now - and whatever challenges you may be facing. I am sure there are countless things you'd rather do then go to the gym, study for that diploma, or stay up late completing lengthy job applications - but how would these fleeting pleasures stand in comparison to the elation you will feel upon achieving the goal on the other end of your small sacrifice?

Speaking of the gym, you are most likely already well aware that your muscles become stronger when exercised. Muscles can also be overworked, leaving them weak and sore while they recover. The same goes for your willpower. Although this means some effort may be on the cards - the good news it is, it doesn't matter where you're at right now - you can become a true willpower bodybuilder if you really put your mind to it.

Some Final Thoughts

To resume, despite the fact that we all face unique challenges in life, we mustn't let this stop us from reaching an optimal level of self-confidence. We have to overcome the tempting mentality that we are mere victims of circumstance, as though we have no authority over our own life and decisions. We must accept that no matter what previous struggles we may have faced, we have no more excuses to seize back control of our present and future.

A simple change in our self-belief and approach to our own capacity to make a change can completely transform our lives: from the goals we set for ourselves and whether or not we take action to achieve them, to how we respond and learn from our failures. For this reason, willpower is crucial - the ability to take action even if you don't feel like it, or don't feel it's fair. This mindset shift is easier to talk about than to actually implement in yourself - but it remains an essential part of any achievement.

It all starts with becoming more confident in ourselves. To not only believe that you can but to decide that you will! If you really want to do it, you already have everything you need.

Training No. 7
Celebrate your successes

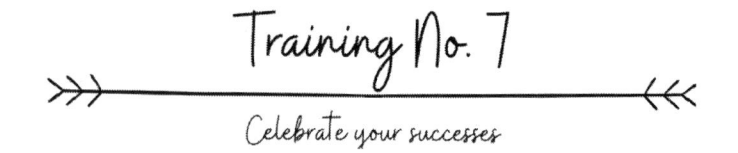

You have reached the final stage of this training.

How did you do?

This last worksheet will help you to get a handle on your personal sense of confidence, acceptance and love for yourself.

In the below worksheet, you will find a list of 15 statements and instructions.

You need to rate your belief in each one on a scale from 0 (not at all) to 10 (completely).

Once you've finished, calculate your average score.

This final score will shed light on your current overall sense of self-esteem/self-confidence on a scale from 0 (I completely dislike who I am) to 10 (I completely like who I am).

Most likely, you still have some room for improvement. So, in order to try to improve your score, respond to the following question:

What would need to change in order to move up one point on the rating scale?

For example, if you rated yourself a 5 what would need to happen for you to be at a 6?

And then take it from there!

I strongly recommend that after finishing this book, you repeat this training after a month. Live your life with an effort to follow the guidance within these pages in the meantime, and trust me - you will find how the overall score will increase over time.

Celebrate your successes

	Rating
1. I like the way I look	1 2 3 4 5 6 7 8 9 10
2. I am just as valuable as other people	1 2 3 4 5 6 7 8 9 10
3. I would rather be me than someone else	1 2 3 4 5 6 7 8 9 10
4. I know my positive qualities	1 2 3 4 5 6 7 8 9 10
5. I'm not afraid to make mistakes	1 2 3 4 5 6 7 8 9 10
6. I am good at solving problems	1 2 3 4 5 6 7 8 9 10
7. I am happy to be me	1 2 3 4 5 6 7 8 9 10
8. I can handle criticism	1 2 3 4 5 6 7 8 9 10
9. I love trying new things	1 2 3 4 5 6 7 8 9 10
10. I respect myself	1 2 3 4 5 6 7 8 9 10
11. I love myself even when others reject me	1 2 3 4 5 6 7 8 9 10
12. I believe in myself	1 2 3 4 5 6 7 8 9 10
13. I feel good when I get compliments	1 2 3 4 5 6 7 8 9 10
14. I focus on my successes and not my failures	1 2 3 4 5 6 7 8 9 10
15. I am proud of my accomplishments	1 2 3 4 5 6 7 8 9 10

Which is your Rating?

| 1 | 2 | 3 | 4 | 5 | 6 | 7 | 8 | 9 | 10 |

I completely dislike who I am   I completely like who I am

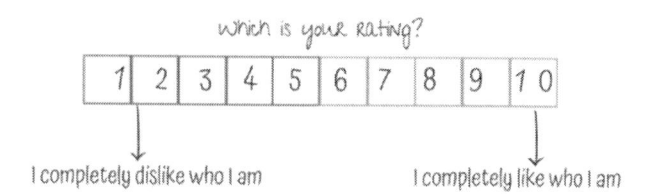

What would you need to change in oRdeR to move up one point on the Rating scale?

Conclusions

You did it - you completed my self-confidence training, and you should now feel filled with a new sense of excited enthusiasm to grab your life with both hands and to propel yourself into a whole new realm of possibility now laid out for you.

Just to have a quick recap of what you should now take away from this book:

Understand your own control over your self-confidence, as well as what the less-understood but equally crucial terms of self-efficacy, self-esteem, and self-acceptance all mean.

Set goals, both for the long-term and the short-term, that are both personal to you and realistic. Learn to prioritize and strategize to make sure you follow through with your plans.

Shift to a positive mindset of growth and responsibility and banish negative, counterproductive thinking. Look after your physical and mental wellbeing in order to build the emotional strength to face life head-on.

Face up to your fears and realize that you are capable of more than you thought, and what was scaring you away from success isn't as you thought. Turn your fear of the unknown into curiosity.

Take action to kickstart those dreams into a reality and discover what you are really capable of. Seize the opportunities provided by the psychological habit loop - without falling prey to its dangers.

Embrace failure and use it as a guide and a teacher rather than a dead-end or permission to give up. Understand that failures are an inevitable part of the journey - and overcoming them an integral part of your success story.

Believe in yourself and don't use external circumstances or past experiences as an excuse - whatever your past, you got this! But remember that self-confidence is about balance and integrity.

The aim of this book was to nurture a genuine and robust belief in yourself, that you can lean on throughout the peaks and troughs of your life journey. To encourage you not to give up on your aspirations, even when they appear to be distant dreams. To have the success you crave and deserve, despite the inevitable obstacles and failed attempts, you must overcome along the way. And ultimately, to live a happy and satisfying life where you feel you can truly be yourself and feel comfortable with that.

Of course, I encourage you to refer back to the chapters covering the specific topics as they become recurrently relevant in your real-life situations. Next time you are in the market for setting goals, or seeking strength to overcome a particularly gut-wrenching failure, for example, please do have a flick back through and use this book as your own portable therapist. I trust that it can offer you some comfort and also be a source of motivation when you need it the most.

After all, we all could use a little reminder here and there how strong and capable we truly are once we lock in a mindset of positivity and growth, and are able to both acknowledge and embrace our weaknesses, fears, and failures. We must remember, above all else, that no one's life is easy or without setbacks. As such, to expect this of yours is unrealistic and only sets you up for disappointment. We shouldn't regard ourselves as invincible, but neither should we see ourselves as victims. Believing in yourself - as you will by now have gathered - is paramount when it comes to living a fulfilled life, where you feel mentally strong, capable, able to set meaningful goals for yourself, take action in spite of your fears and challenges, and overcome your failures. However, I must remind you that although I could (and often do!) sing the praises of self-confidence all day, I also can't stress enough the importance of balance. You can always have too much of a good thing.

Being overly confident - in other words, believing yourself to be *superior* to others rather than equal - leads to damaged relationships and a false belief that you are indestructible. This will only harm you in the long run. People falling into this trap may not take responsibility for their own mistakes and will push others away, or make harmful decisions as a result.

And so, we shouldn't believe our value or abilities to be inferior to everyone else's, but we also shouldn't regard ourselves as superior. Even when the success and improved self-belief starts to roll in after following the carefully curated advice between these pages, don't forget to keep yourself humble. Remember that the sustainable and constructive self-confidence that you should be aiming for is about balance. Do not overestimate yourself, but at the same time, allow yourself to feel joy due to your achievements. This will help you to put in place new targets in line with your skills - to feel pride, but also gratitude and humility.

Don't get me wrong: self-confidence is essential for personal growth and life satisfaction. It's no wonder that new books and articles on how to boost it are published every day. That being said, some authors neglect to talk about the negative side of being overconfident; I don't want to make that same mistake. It's important to clarify that extremes are always dangerous and likely to cause harm - so just as a very low level of confidence is cause for concern, a very high level is too. And swinging from one extreme to another won't help either: it's a stable, consistent, and hard-to-budge sense of inner-confidence that doesn't spike or crash, that we should be aiming for.

We may feel more confident some days than others. This is, of course, a normal part of life's fluctuations. But the goal is for your self-confidence not to vary *too much*. It should preferably always stay within a manageable and healthy window, come what may.

Overall, the resounding difference between a healthily high level of self-confidence, and an unhealthy, over-confident attitude, is that the former is the belief that you are just as capable and worthy as everyone else, whereas the latter leads you to believe that you are actually *more* capable and worthy. On the other end of the scale, if you are grappling with a victim mentality, you underestimate your capability to take action in your life. Both of these extremes are toxic and can greatly damage your relationships and success.

So get to know and believe in yourself no matter what - but recognize and believe in others too. Your journey to self-confidence and self-acceptance isn't only yours - but a universal journey we all must take.

Some Final Thoughts

I must reiterate that you already have all that is required within you to shape your life into the one you've always wanted. But you must make an effort to sharpen your existing skills, get to know yourself - flaws and all - very deeply, and to foster the self-confidence to see you through. Simply "getting by" and letting life happen to you without taking any real control over it - especially if you then use those energy conserves to complain incessantly about how things aren't going your way - is such a waste of your potential and a drain on your self-esteem.

You must now take the building blocks offered in this book to establish a healthy and balanced sense of self-confidence to make you feel equipped to face your life and your personal struggles head-on.

At the beginning of this journey, I promised you that if you overcome the self-doubt, you're currently grappling with - and you put in all the necessary effort, you will be able to reach your goals. I pledged to show you how to tap into a new realm of self-confidence to transform your passive life into an active one. Please take away the lasting message that if you live every single moment at your full capacity (while taking the necessary rest and self-care measures, of course!), then you won't have any regrets. You will be sure that you achieved your potential - you went down every avenue you wished, and you tried everything you wanted.

By now, I trust you have a deep understanding of how nurturing your self-confidence as your one true source of motivation is the key to life satisfaction of achieving success. Your self-confidence, when sustained at a healthy level, will propel you into the heights and straight through the lows. It will enable you to see clearly the perfect imperfection of life, and the inevitable twists and turns of your own. It will keep you feeling strong and capable when challenged, and positive and determined to overcome your setbacks. It will help you to present your true self to the world - not just the shy fraction of your true personality that is all you previously dared to reveal to the outside world.

You will feel more empowered. More authentic. More daring to set your bar high, set the goals you need to dive into the future you want, face up to your fears, laugh off your failures, and above all - believe in yourself no matter what.

So get to know who you really are - what you really want out of your life, and how you will take action to get it. You are your own greatest advocate if you allow yourself to be! But recognize and believe in others too. Your journey to self-confidence and self-acceptance isn't only yours - but a universal mission we all must take.

To finish with an apt quote by American author and activist, Marianne Williamson:

'Who am I to be brilliant, gorgeous, talented, fabulous?'
Actually, who are you not to be?

References

4 D Diagnostic Tool. (N.d.). Retrieved from http://lauraleerose.com/4%20D%20Diagnostic%20Tool.pdf

A. (n.d.). 7 Ways to Give up the Victim Mentality and Live with Confidence. Retrieved from https://www.purposefairy.com/67135/7-ways-to-give-up-the-victim-mentality-and-live-with-confidence/

Adult health. (n.d.). Retrieved from https://www.mayoclinic.org/healthy-lifestyle/adult-health/in-depth/self-esteem/art-20047976

Azimy, R. (2020, March). The Power of Positive Thinking. Retrieved from https://medium.com/illumination/the-power-of-positive-thinking-88a120ae2a57

Behance, Inc. (2019, February 27). The Thinking Mindset vs. The Doing Mindset: Pick One (And Only One). Retrieved from https://99u.adobe.com/articles/7240/the-thinking-mindset-vs-the-doing-mindset-pick-one-and-only-one

Belin, A. (2020, April 22). How to Crush Your Lack of Motivation and Always Stay Motivated. Retrieved from https://www.lifehack.org/articles/communication/how-to-forever-cure-to-your-lack-of-motivation.html

Bilanich, B. (2012, July 30). Fear is the Enemy of Self Confidence. Retrieved from https://www.fastcompany.com/1084542/fear-enemy-self-confidence

Building confidence. (2020). Retrieved from https://www.skillsyouneed.com/ps/confidence.html

Changing Habits – (2020, March 16). Retrieved from https://learningcenter.unc.edu/tips-and-tools/changing-habits/

Cherry, K. (2019, July). When Too Much Self-Confidence Is a Bad Thing. Retrieved from https://www.verywellmind.com/can-you-have-too-much-self-confidence-4163364

Cuddy, A. (2010). Your body language may shape who you are. Retrieved from https://www.ted.com/talks/amy_cuddy_your_body_language_may_shape_who_you_are/transcript?language=en

Dayton, D. (2018, November). Definition of Short Term Goal Setting. Retrieved from https://careertrend.com/definition-short-term-goal-setting-36343.html

Dulin, D. (2019, June). 15 killer action steps to building self confidence. Retrieved from https://www.unfinishedsuccess.com/building-self-confidence/

Embrace the Benefits of Safe Failure. (n.d.). Retrieved from https://learningsolutionsmag.com/articles/1355/embrace-the-benefits-of-safe-failure

Galli, A. (2018, June 21). How to Be Outrageously Consistent | 7 Tips to Be Consistently Consistent. Retrieved from https://medium.com/the-mission/how-to-be-outrageously-consistent-7-tips-to-be-consistently-consistent-a32fd1c0a250

Growth Mindset: The Surprising Psychology of Self-Belief. (2019). Retrieved from https://nickwignall.com/growth-mindset/

Hayes, S. (n.d.). How To Take Action When You Don't Wanna. Retrieved from https://www.psychologytoday.com/us/blog/get-out-your-mind/201802/how-take-action-when-you-don-t-wanna

How Setting Intentions Improved My Confidence | HealthyPlace. (2015, October 9). Retrieved from https://www.healthyplace.com/blogs/buildingselfesteem/2015/10/how-setting-intentions-improved-my-confidence

How to Learn From Your Mistakes: And Put Those Lessons Into Practice. (n.d.). Retrieved from https://www.mindtools.com/pages/article/learn-from-mistakes.htm

How to maintain confidence after experiencing failure - Quora. (n.d.). Retrieved from https://www.quora.com/How-do-you-maintain-confidence-after-experiencing-failure

https://www.skillsyouneed.com/ps/confidence.html. (2020). Retrieved from https://www.skillsyouneed.com/ps/confidence.html

HuffPost is now a part of Verizon Media. (n.d.-a). Retrieved from https://www.huffpost.com/entry/embrace-your-own-reality-its-the-key-to-happiness_b_7102544

HuffPost is now a part of Verizon Media. (n.d.-b). Retrieved from https://www.huffpost.com/entry/realistic-optimist_b_8018530
I.O. (2017). 5 Reasons Why You Must Develop Your Self-Confidence. Retrieved from https://magazine.vunela.com/5-reasons-why-you-must-develop-your-self-confidence-7d69523a9c7e
Josa, C. (2018, July 27). Imposter Syndrome: It's Not All In Your Head. Retrieved from http://www.clarejosa.com/inspiration/clear-out-your-blocks/imposter-syndrome-not-head/
K.W. (2015, October). Self-Confidence and Self-Esteem Aren't the Same Thing. Retrieved from https://lifehacker.com/self-confidence-and-self-esteem-aren-t-the-same-thing-1737949859
Lesson Plan 5: Stepping Out of My Comfort Zone. (n.d.). Retrieved from http://www.successfullives.co.uk/wp-content/uploads/Teacher-Lesson-Plan-5-Stepping-Out-of-My-Comfort-Zone.pdf
Mohr, T. (2019, June 12). Bringing Curiosity to Fear. Retrieved from https://www.taramohr.com/dealing-with-fear/bring-curiosity-to-fear/
Moore, A. (n.d.). How to Activate Extreme Self-Confidence and Destroy Chronic Anxiety and Fear. Retrieved from https://thriveglobal.com/stories/how-to-activate-extreme-self-confidence-and-destroy-chronic-anxiety-and-fear/
Moran, G. (n.d.). Yes, you'll fail. This is how you'll actually learn from it. Retrieved from https://www.fastcompany.com/90314749/the-right-way-to-fail
Moulder, H. (n.d.). How to Set Goals for Building Self-Confidence and Fulfillment. Retrieved from https://www.coursecorrectioncoaching.com/how-to-set-goals-for-building-self-confidence-and-fulfillment/#Goals_and_Self-Confidence
Muller, D. (2020). How to remove cortisol from the body naturally. Retrieved from https://www.medicalnewstoday.com/articles/322335
Overcoming Fear of Failure: Facing Fears and Moving Forward. (n.d.). Retrieved from https://www.mindtools.com/pages/article/fear-of-failure.htm
Pflug, T. (2019, August 30). How Taking Action is Helping You Grow Your Self-Confidence. Retrieved from https://personal-development-zone.com/taking-action-self-confidence/
Seltzer Ph.D., L. F. (2010, August). The Path to Unconditional Self-Acceptance. Retrieved from https://www.psychologytoday.com/ie/blog/evolution-the-self/200809/the-path-unconditional-self-acceptance
Setting Realistic Timeframes for Goals. (n.d.). Retrieved from https://www.achieve-goal-setting-success.com/timeframes.html
Shrestha, P. (2019, June 16). Yerkes - Dodson Law. Retrieved from https://www.psychestudy.com/general/motivation-emotion/yerkes-dodson-law
SMART Goals 101. (n.d.). Retrieved from https://www.briantracy.com/blog/personal-success/smart-goals/
Steven Stosny, Ph.D. (2014, June). How Much Do You Value Yourself? Retrieved from https://www.psychologytoday.com/ie/blog/anger-in-the-age-entitlement/201406/how-much-do-you-value-yourself
Strategies for Learning from Failure. (n.d.). Retrieved from https://hbr.org/2011/04/strategies-for-learning-from-failure
The Dangers of Excessively High Self-Esteem. (2019). Retrieved from https://exploringyourmind.com/the-dangers-of-excessively-high-self-esteem/
The Habit Loop | Habitica Wiki | Fandom. (n.d.). Retrieved from https://habitica.fandom.com/wiki/The_Habit_Loop
The Science & Psychology Of Goal-Setting 101. (2020, February). Retrieved from https://positivepsychology.com/goal-setting-psychology/
Using the Law of Attraction for Joy, Relationships, Money & Success. (n.d.). Retrieved from https://www.jackcanfield.com/blog/using-the-law-of-attraction/
What is Self-Confidence? + 9 Ways to Increase It. (2020). Retrieved from https://positivepsychology.com/self-confidence/
Why Self-Confidence Is More Important Than You Think. (2018). Retrieved from https://www.psychologytoday.com/ie/blog/shyness-is-nice/201809/why-self-confidence-is-more-important-you-think

Why we should embrace failure. (n.d.). Retrieved from https://believeperform.com/why-we-should-embrace-failure/

wikiHow. (2018, September 27). How to Build Confidence by Facing Your Fears. Retrieved from https://www.wikihow.com/Build-Confidence-by-Facing-Your-Fears

Zetlin, M. (2020a, February 6). Here's How to Tell the Difference Between a Truly Confident Person and an Insecure One Who's Bluffing. Retrieved from https://www.inc.com/minda-zetlin/never-admitting-youre-wrong-confidence-insecurity-mistakes.html

Zetlin, M. (2020b, February 6). Want to Be More Confident? 9 Ways to Overcome Your Own Fears. Retrieved from https://www.inc.com/minda-zetlin/9-ways-being-afraid-can-make-you-a-stronger-leader.html

Book 2

Stop Overthinking

The Complete guide to declutter your mind, ease anxiety, and turn off your intensive thoughts.

Overcome indecision and procrastination for a stress-Free Life.

For men and women.

written by Sebastian O'Brien

Table of contents

Introduction	177
Chapter 1 What exactly is overthinking?	184
Chapter 2 How to focus on your present	206
Chapter 3 How to get rid of mental junk	227
Chapter 4 I'm not my thoughts, I'm what I do	245
Chapter 5 Perfectionism vs excellence	263
Chapter 6 Indecisiveness and how to fight it	284
Chapter 7 Procrastination cure	306
Chapter 8 Mindfulness meditation	327
Conclusions	347

Introduction

Do you ever feel like you overthink every single thing? So much so that it has become an obsession - clouding your judgment and preventing you from doing what you want in life - taking risks or reaching your potential?

Since you picked up this book, I would assume that you are no stranger to lying awake at night ruminating over the happenings of that day - or even something you did months or years ago. Your mind may be weighed down with regrets, "what-if"s, or niggling worries that actually blur your vision from seeing whatever is right in front of you. As a result, you are living in the past or future, and missing the most precious gift of all - the present.

You are not alone. As humans, we are all profound and reflective thinkers - and of course, this isn't a bad thing! Quite the contrary - this is what has allowed our species to progress thus far - it has been our ticket to civilization - to inventions, to progress, to modern life as we know it. This ability to think beyond the here and now, to reflect, to plan, to self-criticize.

However, thanks to this evolutionary quirk that just so happened to nudge our species into the stone age and beyond, today, many of us get into the habit of thinking every tiny detail and ruminating over every risk or setback. So much so, that we struggle to enjoy our lives, or dare to dive into the future that we want.

Not to mention that overthinking can even lead to anxiety and depression if not taken care of, as it can seriously hinder our mental clarity and emotional wellbeing.

But how do you know if you're an overthinker?

Here are 8 tell-tale signs:

1. You replay embarrassing moments in your head over and over again…

2. You have trouble sleeping because it feels like your brain won't slow down or switch off.

3. You are often asking yourself "what if"… "What if I had chosen the other option?" "What if I fail?" "What if I'm not good enough?"

4. You spend a lot of time thinking about the potential hidden meanings behind things – "Is she not replying because of something I said?" "When I said that, did he think I was stupid?" "Were they looking at me like that because they were talking about me?"

5. You ruminate over previous conversations you had with people, and think about all the things you could have or should have said.

6. You constantly relive mistakes, criticism, or moments that bring back negative feelings in your head.

7. You are sometimes not fully aware of what's going on around you because you're too busy obsessing over what happened in the past, or what may happen in the future.

8. You spend a lot of time worrying about things outside of your control.

Does any of this sound familiar? If so, then stay with me!

The research is pretty clear — overthinking can be harmful both for mental and physical health (not to mention life satisfaction and success!) and actually doesn't help to prevent or solve your problems. Psychological research on the subject has revealed the following concerning statistics:

- Thanks to modern living, 73% of 25-35 year-olds, 52% of 45-55 year-olds and 20% of 65-75 year-olds are chronic overthinkers.
- Overthinking contributes to severe depression and anxiety and interferes with problem-solving abilities.
- Overthinking significantly increases the risk of unhealthy eating and drinking habits, and other self-harming behaviors, including smoking and drug abuse.

But fear not - you can learn to let go of this harmful habit. To loosen up a bit, and remember how to have fun. How to sleep at night without obsessively thinking about every "what if" your mind haunts you with. How to make a choice with confidence and feel excited and positive when you think about your future, rather than full of doubt.

The secret? You need to reset your approach to life. To learn how to be okay with not being perfect, with making mistakes, and with not always knowing exactly where the future will lead. Scrap that - to not only "be okay" with all of these things, but to realize that this is what keeps life interesting - and above all, a learning and self-development experience. Many of us think we want perfection and predictability - but this would get boring pretty quickly if we had our way!

And so, through some lessons, examples, and tips - I invite you to delve into some of the latest psychological research and tactics when it comes to this ever-increasing global disease that is overthinking - and remember how to switch off from time to time, to ensure we don't burn our poor overworked brains out.

Whether you're a workaholic, a perfectionist parent or partner, or tend to obsess about your productivity and set very high standards for yourself, setting your head into a constant spin - then this book may be just what you need. We are all overthinkers at times, but the sooner you learn some coping mechanisms to not let obsessive worrying or racing thoughts disrupt your life or goals - the better.

To briefly introduce myself and my background, my name is Sebastian O'Brien. I was born in Ireland, 1980 and have worked as a Psychotherapist and counselor for many years. I support a whole range of individuals who are struggling with overthinking and anxiety - both through my face-to-face consultations and now, much to my excitement, via my book! This has always been a dream of mine - to be able to reach countless more individuals who are grappling with these all-too-common mental hurdles, by sharing my years of experience and research in an accessible way through the pages you hold before you.

Here's the thing: the link between overthinking and mental health complications is a chicken-and-egg type of situation. Overthinking is linked to psychological problems, like depression and anxiety - but do we overthink because we are anxious and depressed, or are we anxious and depressed because we overthink? Most likely, it actually goes both ways. And this is why this is such a toxic vicious cycle. Once you are in it, it's hard to break out. Many spend years or even decades on a perpetually spinning hamster wheel of thinking, and anxiety, and more thinking, and more anxiety...

On top of that, "analysis paralysis" is a real problem. This means that the more options you feel you have before you, the more you think. And the more you think, the more trapped you feel. So much choice that you feel that the choice is actually taken away from you. Yes, French philosophers have been talking about this for some time now, but in this increasingly materialistic and overwhelming world, it is more relevant than ever this overwhelmed feeling many of us get as a symptom of a modern (and often pretty successful) life.

We all have plenty on our plate - this is a fact of life. I am, of course, not claiming that I can fix all the problems on your mind. However, what I can do is teach you how to better approach your problems, so that they become less of an emotional burden. This, in turn, will allow you to be better able to fix them or manage them for yourself.

If you overcome the urge to ruminate and overthink every single worry or "what-if" in your life - you will be able to overcome your self-destructive and self-punishing mental habits for yourself, to make you better equipped and more emotionally resilient to handle the inevitable turbulence that will come your way. This, I can promise you.

Ultimately, I will show you how to tap into a new realm of inner peace and mental clarity to transform the way you problem-solve and approach your life's challenges. Live in the moment, and you won't waste it obsessing over past mistakes or future threats. Learning how to think clearly and give your mind the rest and space it needs could be your ticket to mental wellness and contentment.

Chapter 1

What exactly is overthinking?

The Ancient Greek stoic thinker, Socrates was perhaps onto something when he proclaimed:

'the unexamined life is not worth living.'

However, I would add that the overly examined life isn't one I would personally recommend either. As with most things in life, it's all about balance.

And then there's Descartes' 'I think therefore I am,' mantra - that didn't catch on as much as it did for nothing! Thinking is - though I don't mean to claim this groundbreaking idea as my own - pretty darn useful. And by calling out overthinking, I do not by any means wish to discourage deep thinking in itself. Rather, as with any addictive and self-destructive behavior, overthinking is harmful. It takes what are perhaps the most valuable abilities we possess as a species - critical thinking and imagination - and turns them up to 100, burning out our minds and our emotional capacity along with it.

In fact, if you have a tendency to overthink, it can be completely ravaging to both your mental and physical processes. It sends the brain's stress response into overdrive, inducing the fight-or-flight response. As a result, your brain and body are flooded with the stress hormones cortisol and adrenaline - and not only during those sporadic and brief periods where danger is imminent, as this response is designed for, but any time your thoughts start to wander into overthinking territory…

In this sense, you could say that Humanity actually evolved to become a species of overthinkers. Despite our cognitive ability putting us literally a head and shoulders above the Animal Kingdom, we still have the same primitive fight or flight mechanism, but now whipped up into a toxic cocktail with our human love of THINKING. Essentially, we are now doomed to 'think ourselves into stress.' Thanks to our ruminating brains - no threat is ever truly gone! The things you lie awake thinking about at night - are any of them an immediate threat to your life? Does thinking about them incessantly ever solve anything?

Since our nervous systems haven't been able to keep up with our newfound thinking abilities - they continue to flood our bodies with the hormones to keep us alert and panicked enough to spring out of harm's way - and so we stay perpetually alert… and perpetually ready to run. Is it any wonder we can't switch off? Or that anxiety, insomnia, and panic disorders are becoming increasingly widespread in the modern world?

We end up physically and emotionally exhausted, oscillating between jittery anxiety and overwhelming, apathetic fatigue, once our body's overused adrenaline supply eventually dries up.

Overthinking explained
Is overthinking a disorder? Why is it bad?

So, to start right at the beginning. What is overthinking? Why does it happen? And what's the difference between rumination, introspection, problem-solving, and self-reflection? I must first clarify that in most cases, although not ideal, overthinking it is not necessarily pathological or cause for medication, and you can work on overcoming it - all you need is the right techniques and advice. However, it does require a thorough understanding of the thought mechanisms, the neurophysiological response, and the triggers - so that you are aware of what overthinking looks like, why you do it, and most importantly - how to stop it in its tracks!

As mentioned, overthinking isn't a disorder or an illness in itself. Rather, it's a trap we all fall into from time to time. And although this means no one is exempt, on a more positive note, it also means no one is cursed with it forever! However, overthinking is still a potentially harmful and self-sabotaging habit that should be taken very seriously, as when an individual can't stop obsessing and irrationally worrying over things in the long term, and regardless of circumstances (in other words, it's not a temporary state due to a particular life event or a temporary concern), it can interfere severely with their mental health and quality of life.

All in all, overthinking is as common as breathing in this modern world of both endless possibility and endless stress. The worries of the world are just one click or swipe away, and our sphere of concern is stretched far beyond its natural limitations - biologically intended only for a select few in your family or tribe. In today's reality of globalization and digital connectivity, we are exposed both to more information and more trauma - and this doesn't go unnoticed by our subconscious. It's a great thing to be able to communicate and receive news from all four corners of the world, but our poor minds are not wired to expand our empathy to such a degree. Therefore, we are not mentally prepared to process so much emotional stimulation and cope with such a fast-paced world. Is it any wonder, then, that our minds tend to spiral out of control if we don't make the required effort to keep ourselves grounded?

Many clients also have complaints of reliving past failures, mistakes, or traumas over and over again; they feel simply unable to move past them, forgive themselves or heal and move on. Many also struggle to stop their relentless worrying about their goals and future tasks - until they feel almost impossible to accomplish. And for others, it's the obsession with what others think of them that keeps them up at night. Did I offend them? did I embarrass myself? What must they think of me? And so on.

So, which one is your poison?

Overall, the obstacle to vanquish is this (perceived) inability to slow down the racing of thoughts, worries or emotions - that only incites a vicious cycle of anxiety and chronic stress. Whatever your demons are, you must work on not allowing them to torment you. I hope to not inspire any further anxiety in you when I say that this will only lead to further mistakes or general unease. In this way, you are not permitting yourself to be calm: to simply experience the present moment (more on that later!) and allow the natural rhythms of your thoughts to flow with ease - unshaken by your intrusive spiraling.

"I'm just problem solving"

The difference between overthinking and problem-solving.

You may be one of those overthinkers that claims it's all just necessary problem-solving. "I can't pretend my problems don't exist," or "someone has to think about these things," may be mantras of yours when having to explain your deep thoughts - either to others or just to yourself. However, it's an easy mistake to make to confuse overthinking with innocent problem-solving. You might convince yourself that letting your worries spin around your mind in this way is productive. However, don't forget that the solution to a problem doesn't tend to come more easily simply by *thinking harder*. In fact, some of our greatest emotional clarity comes from adequate physical and emotional rest and distancing one's worries.

On the topic of overthinking versus problem-solving, Michael D. Yapko, a clinical psychologist in Fallbrook, California, states that 'most people who engage in rumination don't know they're ruminating; they think they're problem-solving - not being able to distinguish between the two is part of the problem. If it doesn't lead to a timely and effective course of specific action, it's rumination.'

Think of it this way: a simple definition of problem-solving is actively looking for the solution to an issue. You will know if you are problem-solving when you notice a decrease in stress as you work on untangling the mess of thoughts you were presented with. On the other hand, overthinking involves over-analysis and rumination (which I will come to next!). This only spurs you to dwell on your worries and prevents you from having the mental capacity to coin a solution for yourself. Overthinking magnifies every minute issue, or even unlikely possibilities - making you focus on the worst-case scenarios as though they are already set in stone.

Indeed, the human mind is cruel like that; the more you think, the more darkness you create for yourself—causing you to be stuck in a state of perpetual anxiety.

The different types of deep thinking

What are rumination, self-reflection, and introspection?

Time for some key terms: rumination, self-reflection, and introspection: but what do these all mean? There is an important difference between rumination - something to be avoided - and the other two - which are to be aimed for. Not all deep thoughts are equal! Of course, with the promise of personal growth and increased creativity, time spent alone to ponder the complexities of your own life can be a positive and productive experience. This opportunity to mull things over can be hugely beneficial to your emotional state and mental clarity, and your saving grace if you are feeling overwhelmed or uncertain. You have a bafflingly complex and powerful brain - so use it! But use it wisely. However, if we are negatively turned against ourselves or become obsessive or compulsive in our thought-processes, then this time spent in reverie can also become dangerous. So how can we be sure what kind of thinking we are engaging in - to make sure that it is not harming us, but nourishing us?

Rumination

Let's begin with rumination - the one to be avoided, being one of the modern human's greatest downfalls. Technically, rumination is simply the technical term for "overthinking," occurring when you become trapped in a negative cycle of circular thinking that can trigger episodes of depression or paranoia. As put by Steve Ilardi, associate professor of Clinical Psychology at the University of Kansas: "rumination involves dwelling repetitively and at length on negative thoughts, often related to failure, rejection, humiliation, loss or retaliation."

I also get behind fellow psychologist Susan Nolen-Hoeksema's definition of rumination as "...repeatedly and passively thinking about the causes or consequences of problems without moving to active problem-solving." For example, ruminating about your weight instead of taking action to change it for the better. Ruminating about what someone thinks of you instead of engaging with them to correct any potential misunderstanding. Or, ruminating about how much you despise your job and yet doing nothing to change your situation. Sound familiar?

The thing is, every person is divided between a healthy attitude toward themselves - you know, that goal-directed and life-affirming voice that takes over sometimes, when you're feeling your best, keeping your head above water, your worries at bay, and your eyes on the prize? But then there's the self-destructive side that we all must also manage. That critical, paranoid, and suspicious voice that lures you away from your goals and squashes your self-esteem every chance it gets. Making you believe you shouldn't or you can't. That people think badly of you or that you are a failure. This inner critic can take over our thinking if we don't manage to get a hold over it, which is what leads to rumination.

However, when this less desirable side of our consciousness is kept in check, we are capable of having a more positive and self-reflection, realistic and yet untarnished by our negative thoughts.

The trap is that in-depth thought DOES often lead to useful and necessary insights. In a sense, by thinking deeply about our life and how we go about navigating it, we are walking on a knife's edge - one slip and we tumble into the hard-to-escape depths of rumination. Just as with anything, if you get used to reaping positive results, you will repeat the activity. This is called the habit loop, and I discussed it at length in my previous book, Self-Confidence Training. These behaviors then become associated with benefits and lodged into our mind as go-to activities. As such, they tend to be very tricky to change.

But rumination won't get you anywhere - as it's like getting stuck. Your wheels are spinning furiously, but you just won't budge...

Self-Reflection

So what can we turn to instead of rumination during those quiet moments where we really have a chance to consider how we are living our lives? Enter: self-reflection.

Essentially, self-reflection is exactly what it implies - an ability to reflect upon yourself in a clear-headed and objective way. When you engage in true self-reflection, you really see yourself: your actions, the way you behave and interact with others, and how you could work on your current attributes. Self-reflection means seeing yourself for who you are.

This may sound simple - of course you can see yourself, right? Don't we all already know "who we are"? Well, I assure you that most people really don't. We may know what our reflection looks like in the mirror. We may know our first name, our surname, heck - we know our mother's maiden name and the time and date that we were born. You know your qualifications and you know (at least, I hope!) how to do your job. But do you know what lies beneath all of that? When you take away what anyone can find on your birth certificate, passport, resume, or social media page - what is left? Because there is, of course, more to you than all of that… but what?

Don't worry - the mere realization of this is the first big step towards a more positive way of processing your thoughts.

Introspection

At this stage, it's time to take our self-reflection even further. To not only look at ourselves in this way, but to then go on to delve deeper behind the surface and carry out a more thorough self-analysis. This is where introspection comes in.

Introspection is the process of healthy self-examination and self-discovery, which is a crucial first step when it comes to establishing healthier mental and emotional habits. Essentially, introspection is the act of "checking in" with yourself as you would a dear friend - to see where you're at emotionally. When you take this valuable time to be introspective, we must adopt a curious, open-minded, accepting, and self-compassionate attitude. Then think about what you would like to challenge in yourself, and how you want to distance yourself from negative influences - either from your current situation, or from your past. In this way, you will be able to give your life and goals more meaning and more intentional direction, yet without falling victim to your inner-critic - which only serves to hold you back.

You may feel as though you are exploring something; considering new perspectives and deeper meanings behind your thoughts, feelings, and actions. You feel like you have a direction, a purpose, and are heading directly to the answers and awareness you seek. Conversely, rumination feels like going round in circles, and sinking deeper into distress. And so, to avoid tipping over into rumination territory, I strongly encourage people to develop self-compassion and self-awareness. Compassion so that you can be more encouraging and forgiving to yourself and keep your thoughts constructive and forward-thinking, and awareness so that you can recognize for yourself when your thoughts are becoming self-sabotaging, and so you can pull yourself out of rumination's grip when need be.

In essence, introspection is the "next one up" of self-reflection, if you will. It involves not only the observation of the self, but also the examination of one's own mental and emotional state of mind. As such, introspection is a deeply personal and even philosophical act of self-analysis, where you analyze your thoughts, behaviors and beliefs for what they are - a reflection of the experiences that formed you since birth.

When overthinking becomes dangerous for your mental health

Could this habit stem from your childhood?

Some mental health diagnoses have overthinking as a key element - such as post-traumatic stress disorder (PTSD), panic disorder, various anxiety disorders, or severe phobias. However, for the vast majority of us, overthinking is simply a part of life - not an indication of an illness - and something we can manage all on our own once we discover how. That being said, overthinking is still harmful - even for the healthiest of minds.

A recent study found that when people overthink after a stressful experience, since they don't give their already-exhausted mind a break after the trauma, forcing it to replay the turmoil over and over, it takes them longer to recover emotionally. On the other hand, by using constructive tactics such as distraction or mindfulness meditation, individuals were shown to psychologically heal a lot better from their past struggles.

Other research revealed that people with a higher tendency to overthink experience "exaggerated and prolonged increases in their blood pressure and heart rate in response to mental stress." This is hugely concerning and can contribute to long-term blood pressure and, thus, a greater risk of cardiovascular complications over time.

And as a secondary consequence of overthinking, there are various harmful behaviors we feel more inclined to engage in as a consequence of our body's reaction to stress. For instance, overeating high-sugar and high-fat foods in order to replicate the serotonin ("happy hormone") our worn out brains are lacking - or to satisfy our survival instinct's cravings for high-calorie sustenance as it believes you are in an emergency situation where food may be scarce.

Then there's the overconsumption of alcohol, smoking, or the use of recreational drugs - all of which don't need too much explaining, as it's common knowledge how we can all-too-easily become dependent on any drug that offers our anxious minds some respite - no matter how damaging they are do the rest of our bodies. This just illustrates how much stress and overthinking really gets to us! We literally sacrifice our physical health in order to try and feel some temporary peace.

Finally, there are the health consequences such as an increased risk of depression, anxiety, and insomnia - all of which you are at a much higher risk of if you are an overthinker, and which can change your entire outlook on life for the worse. This, of course, can also lead to further health problems down the road.

So no, it's not all in your head. Overthinking can actually negatively impact every part of your body.

The Gender Bias

Here's an interesting element to the overthinking conversation I simply couldn't leave out - how your gender may affect your rumination and stress tendencies. Although, stereotypically, - women have an easier time with introspection and self-reflection than men - being considered the more emotionally attuned of the sexes as a general rule (which could be thanks to their psychological hardwiring as the nurturers and empathises of the species) - whether related or not, they also have a harder time with rumination.

This isn't to say that all women are ruminators, or are more so than their male peers - but it is a fact that if you're a woman, you're at a higher risk of becoming a chronic overthinker… And according to recent scientific research, women are shown to ruminate more often than men do. Maybe there's some truth behind the age-old stereotype that women hone in on the details, whereas men tend to focus on the overall picture?

Other research suggests that women and men have tendencies to ruminate about different things. For instance, men are reported to overthink about work and finances. On the other hand, women are more sensitive to conflict and the illness or death of loved ones as their rumination triggers. Again, this research is both controversial and interesting. It sheds light on how our biology and sociology can impact what we prioritize and fear most in life.

It begs the question: is it the tendency to ruminate itself that women are more prone to, or simply the more social and relationship-focused priorities of most women that can more easily take them down rumination road?

Some psychologists propose that these disparities are rooted in different social statuses, life conditions, and inequalities that still take hold of our societies. For instance, the subconscious beliefs that we are conditioned with from childhood that men should be financially successful providers, and women should be nurturing, and live for their bonds with others. But I'm not here to argue whether these societal norms are right, wrong, natural, or completely made up - I'm just here to tell you that they exist - whether or not you personally subscribe to them! And so, even the most forward-thinking men and women can fall prey to these gendered insecurities, and our data on rumination is shaped as a result.

Of course, all of this could either be a result of nature, nurture, or most likely - a combination of the two. From our hormone profiles to our upbringings and how our gender is expected to behave - there are myriad factors whenever a gender discrepancy like this one emerges. All you need to know is that anyone can succumb to rumination - in fact, to some extent, we all do. The key is how you acknowledge and then learn to manage it.

"Tell me about your childhood..."

Similarly, a study in Psychiatry Research found that people who experienced early life stress – such as emotional or sexual abuse or trauma – have an increased likelihood of being more of an overthinker as an adult. It's simply our frazzled mind's attempt to piece things together and make sense of things. But of course, it doesn't always do this successfully. And naturally, early exposure to the bad side of humanity is likely to shape your outlook throughout your life.

If you experienced intense stress early on in life, even before your brain had the chance to fully mature, then this "frazzled" state is even more severe, and so your brain is whirring away, desperately trying to make sense of the senseless in a tragically obsolete exercise.

How to Problem-Solve Without Ruminating

So whatever your gender, social status, or childhood - what can you do to stop overthinking and rumination in its tracks, while still remaining focused on our self-development and self-aware of where we may be able to improve?

Well, instead of replaying past experiences in your mind's eye, make a plan. What can you do to take action about that situation you can't stop thinking about? There's always something - even if it takes some thinking to get there. Perhaps confronting the person who you had a conflict with? Investing in training to make sure you are better prepared for whatever looming tasks is making you shudder? Letting your boss know that you're overworked and setting down some boundaries?

Whatever you decide, you must do to improve your current anguish, write it out as your action plan. Even if you're not ready to take it, simply seeing it in black and white will start the ball rolling.

The mind behind the Huffington Post and Thrive Global, Arianna Huffington, advises setting a particular time for rumination, or "worry time" as she calls it. Perhaps, for example, between 6:00-6:10 pm, after returning from work, but before preparing dinner, you set aside some time to simply THINK. Think about whatever is on your mind, threatening your inner-peace. Think it to death. But then, when the time's up, resume your other activities. You have given these worries their fair share of your attention, and have hopefully gotten your urge to ruminate out of your system. Any more time would be a waste and could lead to spiraling. And so, between these established "worry time" appointments, refuse to give into your rumination: you're too busy doing something else much more worthwhile!

There is a theory that people often "just know" whether their deep thoughts are damaging or productive. You may know that it's the former and continue anyway, but be honest - you know. There is a different feeling that comes along with each one: if you're ruminating, you almost feel guilty about it - like you're indulging in a naughty habit, and yet all it brings you is pain. Yet set out to think things through rationally and strategically, and it seems like something to be proud of. You feel lighter; more full of energy and motivation than you did before - even if no huge revelation comes from it. You simply know in your gut that you're on the right track.

So how do you distinguish whether you're in a pessimistic overthinking mode, or realistic problem-solving - to prepare for future obstacles?

Whether you're ruminating over a workplace matter, or stressing yourself out over a family issue, the key is to ask yourself whether there is any method or strategy behind those racing thoughts. Are you genuinely making an effort to piece together the components of your dilemma in a clear-headed and solution-oriented way, or simply allowing your panic to take over and scramble your perspective even further, only increasing your anguish over the situation?

Make your thinking more productive and less destructive by being aware of when you are investing more time than necessary or mentally healthy - thinking about a particular situation on your mind. If you're problem-solving - in other words, calmly and strategically mulling over the issue with your focus set on how to solve and move past it - then, by all means, keep going. However, if it turns out you are overthinking - chewing over the issue mercilessly but refusing to swallow it and move on - then make an active decision to refuse to waste any more time or mental energy. Cast it out of your mind, at least for now, either by focusing on a more productive task or thought - or, as I will delve into more later on, by practicing mindfulness meditation.

Once you figure out how to swap your overthinking for genuine problem-solving, you can then channel your time and mental energy into productive activities. You'll gather the emotional strength to devote yourself to fixing rather than ruminating over your worries, which will ultimately help you reach your full, uninhibited potential.

Chapter 2

How to focus on your present

Now it's time to refocus. If you really think about it, it becomes clear that most of our overthinking woes boil down to constantly jumping to the past and future. What happened, what could have happened, what might happen... Most of us don't sit there ruminating over what's right before our eyes - the color of the wall or whatever you can see out of the window. No - overthinking is a time-traveling activity. It causes us to look backward, forwards - anywhere but the present moment.

Even if the idea of focusing on the present may seem basic or obvious, it can really make a profound difference to your chronic overthinking habit. This is because living life in the present is essential for our wellbeing. However, we are wired to think continuously, both about the past - which risks triggering depression, self-resentment, and a lack of self-confidence - or to the future - which often sparks the fear of failure, performance anxiety, and unrealistic expectations.

Life must be lived in the present moment so that we are

able to fully enjoy our mental and physical energies in the present and get rid of the weight of overthinking.

Although a bit of a pain at times, this ability to "time travel" with our thoughts is what makes us human. However pensive your cat may look or however quizzical your dog seems as they stare into space - scientists reiterate that it is most likely only humans - with the possible exception of some great apes and sea mammals - who are donned with this cognitive capacity to think about past events, or ponder the future. A cat most likely is thinking about that bird in the sky. A dog is most often thinking about the fun or food they are or are not having. Humans, on the other hand, lose this primitive stream of consciousness shortly after infancy.

If we clutter our brains, and thus our lives, with painful memories, feelings, and worries, there's little room for anything more positive. To improve your state of mind, you must realize that it's your choice whether to hold onto resentment, bitterness, or even fear. Although we often can't choose whether we experience these feelings as they inevitably come and go, gripping onto them as many of us do, is entirely our decision - even if we often don't see it that way.

Humans: The Mental Time-Travellers

You could say overthinking is part of the human condition, and I would agree with this sentiment to a certain extent - as I believe it is a part of the modern human condition. Let me explain: as touched upon in the first chapter, the human body's issue with stress is linked to our ancient stress response - which evolved not only when we had a whole different lifestyle containing threats far-removed from office politics, mortgage worries, and marital quarrels - but let's not forget that we had a more primitive brain.

Back then, our ancestors were led primarily by the hippocampus - but now our brains have evolved to have a prefrontal cortex too. What does that mean? Well, it means that we now have the ability to look to the past and to the future - as well as think about whatever happens to be in a periphery at a given time. To consider alternative decisions to take, fabricate alternative scenarios in our head, and contemplate our own existence and identity.

And thanks to this curious combination of biology and sociology, we all overthink things at times. We are wired to flee imminent dangers like an animal is, but also to contemplate more abstract concepts, which makes us human. You may be overly concerned with what you said or did to somebody. Did you offend them? Do they hate you now? Alternatively, you may be worried about your performance at school or at work. Or perhaps about your personal relationships. These things would not even be comprehensible to a primitive human – let alone cause for anxiety!

Worse still: today, many of us aren't only often anxious, but we then go on to develop meta-anxiety – that is, anxiety about being anxious. It all starts with worrying about what will happen in the future, which then often takes you down a rumination road of what happened in the past and how things could have been different. Have you noticed what's missing?

Sure, we often get anxious about what is happening in the present moment too, but unless we are under some sort of attack or facing an imminent threat, this is connected to worry of a different time period. We may worry about a look someone gives us or a comment someone makes in the present – but only because of what this may mean in the future. Humans are funny in that way – we just can't seem to stay in the present moment. We expend so much time and energy obsessing over what has or will happen, that we actually lose sight of what is happening right now.

There are also those "what if" scenarios, where you consider what could happen in a variety of circumstances, often paired with an irrational bout of catastrophizing - that is, thinking the worst will happen and letting your imagination run wild with these possibilities. Intrusive or obsessive thoughts are also a common experience. This is where - no matter how much you try to shut down upsetting thoughts or distract yourself from your incessant worries, they keep rearing their ugly heads to monopolize your every waking thought process.

Forgiving the past

Learning from mistakes and practising self-forgiveness.

And so, as humans, we are perhaps doomed to overthink our past and future in this way. After all, the ability to do so has gotten us far! That being said, we need to learn how to turn off this ability so as not to spiral into rumination territory and burn ourselves out. After all, whatever happens in our past - good or (perhaps especially) bad - has the potential to teach us valuable lessons about how to improve our present and future. And so, rather than dwelling on past mistakes or traumas, it is both the self-compassionate and the constructive thing to do to forgive yourself and use this insight for personal growth and self-improvement.

Say, for example, you have two dogs, but one day, one of them passes away. You may spend days, or even weeks, mourning the lost dog. Thinking about how you could have appreciated her more, showed her even more love, somehow done more for her. Then one day, you realize that you don't want to have those feelings again the day the other day dies. Rather than focusing on the dog that you lost, your perception shifts as you suddenly realized you are still blessed with the dog you have. Instead of wallowing over your loss, you channel your mental energy into loving and caring for the other. In this way, you not only distract yourself from rumination over "what ifs," but you also ensure that you learn from any mistakes you made previously and do what you can to avoid similar regrets in the future.

It doesn't matter whether you have or even like dogs – I guarantee there will be some sort of parallel in your life – where you have focused so much on what you don't have, that you forget to enjoy what you do have. Often, the best way to "forgive" or accept the past is to allow the lessons you learned to take shape in your present.

Why do we hold on to the past, specifically? Why is it so easy to ruminate over experiences that only inflict pain, embarrassment, or regret whenever we do? As you will probably know all too well, those who hold onto their past negative experiences often relive the pain they felt back then over and over in their tormented minds. So how can we stop this mental self-harm? How can we get out of our heads and move on?

The only way you can let more positivity into your mind is to make space for it. To lose some baggage, and open yourself up to more positive thoughts and ideas. However, things don't tend to just disappear all on their own. You need to make the commitment for yourself and stick to it. Making a conscious decision to simply "let go" in this way also means accepting that you actually have a choice to let it go - which is an uplifting and empowering revelation itself, that has the potential to change your life in the longer term.

Past = Familiarity

When past memories or worries about the future creep into your stream of consciousness, acknowledge them for just a moment. And then, guide yourself back to the present moment. Some people find this coping mechanism easier with the help of a mantra as a cue, such as 'that was all in the past, and now I'm focused on how to improve my present and future.'

It's so common to get stuck in the past simply because of an inbuilt, irrational fear of the unfamiliar. This causes us to turn to ruminate about the past as a subconscious retreat back into the comfort of certainty. This innate human love of certainty is essentially all about survival. We feel the need to feel secure and aware in the attempt to avoid pain and, ideally, find comfort. And what is more certain than that which has already happened? And so, however negative the past may make you feel at times, one thing it doesn't give you is fear or uncertainty. In the same way, moving on from the past, in a sense, means stepping into the unknown future - choosing to leap somewhat blindly the unknown instead of ruminating over the known. It requires the courage to let go of the familiar - which, even when negative can be subliminally comforting to an anxious mind - and allowing yourself to be vulnerable and open to the future.

The Link Between Memories and Emotion

The other reason it's so difficult to learn how to let go of the past has to do with the way we link emotion to information. They both come from the same part of the brain - the temporal lobe - after all. If you think back to the tragic events of 9/11, you can most likely picture who you were with and what exactly you were doing when you heard about the attack. However, could you recall the 11th June of that same year with the same clarity?

Unless this is also an important day in your personal calendar, then I'm guessing not! Certainly not for every day you have ever lived. This is because our memory is selective when it comes to the details. In order to prioritize meaningful memories from the mundane, our brains don't retain information unless we have feelings attached to it. That's why you may remember fond childhood memories just as clearly as you remember more traumatic past events - but the days where we just did our thing and nothing much happened? Basically - most days we ever live in our lives? They are swiftly forgotten. Maybe even a week after experiencing them!

When information combines with emotion, it creates more of an imprint in your memory. Curiously, some psychologists have also linked this to gender (notice I say gender here - relating to identity and not necessarily to sex chromosomes) as women or anyone with more "feminine" traits have the tendency to attach emotion to more of their memories when compares to their male - or simply more "masculine"-minded - counterparts.

Always have a Plan B

A saying I've gone by since I was young is "failing to prepare is preparing to fail," and harsh as it may sound - it's true! If you feel safe in the knowledge that you have done your research, and always have a plan B in place whenever undertaking a particularly ambitious or risky plan, then a great deal of that anxiety and rumination stemming from the fear of failure will evaporate. Not only that, but focusing your overactive mind on something that is actually constructive to the task at hand, rather than ruminating over what could go wrong, will actually be a great outlet for that nervous mental energy and kill two birds with one stone So I cannot stress this enough - plan, plan and then plan some more!

Realize you can't predict the future

Fighting the fear of failure and trusting your instincts over social expectations.

That being said, you must remember that you cannot - as much as you may believe otherwise - predict the future. Whether it's your career, your relationship, or money worries that are playing on your mind, although you can prepare as best you can to make the best of these things and hope that the future will bring prosperity - we simply cannot know for sure how things will pan out. But don't feel deflated by this - this fact should be liberating! I'm not suggesting you completely throw in the towel and quit caring about the future altogether. However, if you're a chronic overthinker, then you likely worry about things that may not even happen. This is not only a waste of time and mental energy, but it also ruins the present moment! Is it any way to live, constantly looking towards the future with fear and forgetting the blessings you have before you in the present moment?

Just think of all the things you worried about in the past that turned out okay in the long run. Maybe you had similar fears long ago that you can now look back and laugh about. Or alleged failures that you now have the hindsight to realize were necessary to lead you to where you needed to go.

Fear of Failure

The fear of failure can be completely debilitating. It can make you question what you're doing and why you're doing it. Fear can cause you to overthink your plans, and hesitate to actually take that first step into action. It can chip away mercilessly at your self-confidence if you let it leave you feeling utterly incapable of taking the action you need in order to accomplish your goals.

That being said, a certain level of fear can also be motivating. As long as you remain focused on what you hope to achieve, and what you need to do in order to get there - compelling yourself to take the leap despite these niggling fearful feelings, then you can use this nervous energy to actually propel yourself forward, towards your goal. And, as already mentioned, when we fail it can actually be a valuable learning experience if we allow it to be. We all must sometimes fail in order to grow as individuals and become better.

Take Control over your Thoughts (But Not Too Much!)

True contentment and freedom require the realization that what goes on inside your head is your own business - no one can affect it unless you let it. This means that you have the final say when it comes to your emotions. Although you can't always predict what will happen outside of yourself, you can take charge of what happens within, and how you react to external stimuli.

I am, of course, not encouraging you to become akin to some sort of unfeeling robot. Bad things happen to the best of us, and we can react however, we see fit - some instances do call for shouting, crying, or taking some time alone and thinking things through. However, we are often self-destructive in our decisions on how to process bad situations. Yes - notice I said "decisions," because although these reactions may seem outside of our control, they really aren't. As I said, the negative reaction in itself may be inevitable, but how you process it is up to you. You have some flexibility to choose in what way you respond to the tragedy. Do you have a tendency to wallow and basque in your grief, isolating yourself from loved ones? Or, do you let rage get the better of you and lash out at others (or towards yourself) due to the sheer frustration of it all?

Regardless of your particular knee-jerk response to a bad mood or day, there is of course, an absolute right or wrong way – just be aware that some coping mechanisms may do more harm than good, only extending the length of time required for you to heal. The important part is that you are aware of the control that you have. With this awareness, whatever challenge arises next, will feel mentally stronger, more grounded to yourself, and less inclined for your overthinking to spiral out of control - opting instead for more calming and constructive coping mechanisms to your stresses.

That all being said, don't fall into the trap of trying to control your emotions too much. As mentioned, sometimes we all need a good cry or even a good shout - when the occasion calls for it! Pent up emotions or suppressed anger or grief will only linger in your mind until you eventually cannot bottle it up any longer, and it breaks you. Instead, it is better to allow yourself to feel whatever emotions come your way. But make sure you never fully lose touch with your composure or rationality. Express your emotions as a means to communicate or move past them - not simply as a knee-jerk response that will only exacerbate existing worries. Learn to feel your emotions - as you should - but without completely losing your head, so that you can detach yourself from them when the time comes.

Treat your Emotions like the Weather

I like to tell my clients to ride their emotions like the waves that they are - for they will inevitably come and go. The key is to not allow them - whether positive or negative - to completely consume or control you. When I advise controlling your emotions, I don't mean by batting them away and refusing to let them in. Rather, embrace them but then control how you process and move on from them. And remember - just as your negative emotions will come and go, so will your positive ones. Such is the human mind: it never stops! So enjoy your highs, but don't expect them to stay. Be ready for when they are over. But take comfort in the fact that just as your positive emotions are temporary, so are your negative ones - nothing lasts forever - and thank goodness for that! As Ancient Greek Stoic, Seneca wrote:

"They lose the day in expectation of the night, and the night in fear of the dawn."

Indeed, we may not particularly enjoy it when it rains — but we know that this isn't permanent. And so, we may complain - but we put up your umbrella or simply wait indoors for this temporary disturbance to pass. Meanwhile, we are comforted in the knowledge that we will eventually enjoy sunnier days. Our emotions work strangely similar to the weather: both the ups and downs are temporary - to be acknowledged and even responded to with precautionary measures - but always while remembering that no single state will last.

And since the emotions we experience and the ups and downs in our lives aren't permanent in nature, the permanence must come from within. In other words, we must build a reliable level of emotional strength and resilience that will not be weathered by any of life's various storms — even if you do still feel the rain on your skin from time to time!

Trust Your Instincts

The need for acceptance and thus validation from others is a basic human instinct, stemming from our tribal days where being accepted and liked by the rest of your group could mean the difference between life and death. We all want to fit in, to be liked, respected, and to belong to a community of some sort - whether that's our family, our friendship group, or our workplace. As such, we don't always stay true to who we really are as a sort of self-preservation attempt, causing us to doubt our natural instincts and gut reactions to things. Even if we feel like something was the right choice, we overthink what others may think, what others may have done in our situation - and so it is this failure to trust our instincts and own sense of judgment that often leads us down a path of overthinking.

On top of that, it is quite simply impossible to calculate all possible scenarios in the future for all the challenges you will have to face, so it is important to learn to trust your instincts. This is one of the greatest weapons we have available to us, because we can truly determine what our needs are upfront - without too many deliberations. And, most of the time, it gets us out of trouble without us even realizing it. Sure - we are all fallible and may not always get things right - but if you don't get behind your own ideas and trust in your own abilities, then who else will? Something, a little self-belief, is all we need to dig ourselves out of a rumination pit.

You already have everything you need

Finally, it pays to remember that in this materialistic and appearance-obsessed world, we constantly seek happiness and fulfillment from outside ourselves. This is inherently destructive, as it trains us from a young age to believe that our contentment depends on material possessions or milestones we must all achieve. And of course, a worrying amount of our overthinking stems from these insecurities: around wealth, job prospects, superficial or relationship insecurities. For instance:

"If I earned more money, I'd be happy."

"If I had a different body, I'd be happy."

"If I lived in a bigger house, I'd be happy."

"If I were married, I'd be happy."

Does any of this sound familiar?

I must reiterate: there is no material possession, physical attribute, or social or professional status that will truly change your baseline happiness level – the one that can withstand the rainy days. Sure, they may give you a temporary ego boost making you feel better about yourself for a short period of time, but every single thing that brings superficial joy quickly becomes stale – you soon crave something more.

Think of it this way: remember the last time when you felt completely elated? Maybe just after your first date with someone, when you got your first job, or upon receiving a meaningful compliment from someone you admire. Have you noticed that, despite the warm fuzzy feeling or excitement you may feel from these moments, suddenly, these things aren't enough? We all eventually become blasé about the things that once filled us with joy. However, if you discover how to feel content and at peace with whatever you have right now, in the present moment – even If you acknowledge room for improvement and still retain ample motivation to grow and improve on yourself - you will better establish this baseline of contentment I've been talking about, that isn't so easily shaken by the ups and downs of your life.

On top of this, once you stop punishing yourself for your present circumstances - ruminating over the fact that you should have, or have achieved, X, Y, and Z by now, your desires suddenly seem within reach– as you know you'll be happy regardless, so take the crippling self-inflicted pressure away. Your drive to succeed will now be driven by your self-confidence - and not your self-doubt!

The Bottom Line: Find your Flow and be "in the zone"

Have you ever felt completely consumed by the present moment? Most likely, you are engaged in an activity that you're good at. Something that arouses you jets enough to keep you interested, without typing over into anxious territory. Something that calms you just enough to leave you feeling peaceful, but not so much that it leaves you feeling bored or unstimulated. For some, this could be when painting, drawing, reading, writing, cooking, or running. Whatever it is that gets you into this near-meditative and mind-nourishing state, you will be completely engaged with your present. The back-chatter of your mind begins to melt, and any rogue "what if" thoughts are temporarily silenced, as you enjoy the here and now.

Commonly referred to as being "in the zone," this state of mind is known within psychology as the "flow" state. The term was coined by Hungarian scientist, Mihaly Csikszentmihalyi. He became fascinated with the concept when he studied how artists and musicians become almost entranced by their work. Artists, scientists, and athletes alike all recalled similar experiences when engaged in their activity: a state of both heightened senses and yet seemingly incongruous tranquility.

Indeed, this metaphor of "flow" contributes to the overall imagery of water. Most likely because it is our mental equivalent of floating peacefully down a stream - still moving, but gracefully, at ease, and without your body weighing you down as it would do on land. As put by Bruce Lee:

"You must be shapeless, formless, like water. When you pour water in a cup, it becomes the cup. When you pour water in a bottle, it becomes the bottle. When you pour water in a teapot, it becomes the teapot. Water can drip, and it can crash. Become like water, my friend."

By living in the present, you must assimilate. Become at ease. Although you are alert and often hard at work, you are still relaxed, calm, and ready for wherever the water may take you.

As you strive to let go of your past and quit overthinking your future while you're at it, it helps to also identify something you are aiming for that is greater than yourself. This could be your family, your career development, or even your own mental health or self-discovery journey. Whatever it is, having a motive really does matter. This is what gives us purpose and a reason to continue despite any setbacks or hardships. It reminds us that behind all of the responsibilities, the mistakes, and what-ifs, we are simply flawed, well-intentioned humans trying to get by. No, we can't get it perfect every time. And no - our futures can't be perfect either! But we find the courage and the humility to carry on anyway, trying our best but accepting our mistakes.

And so, we owe it to ourselves to refocus on the present moment. To get out of our heads at least some of the time, and remember to just be – to drink life in as it is currently looking rather than wasting it by mourning what could or should have been.

Chapter 3

How to get rid of mental junk

A key part of tackling any overthinking addiction is limiting unnecessary information in the brain and organizing the justified thoughts you are left in a more efficient way. Of course, you must not - and simply cannot - stop thinking altogether. Rather, the secret is to learn how to think with clarity and focus, ditching any mental junk getting in the way of your important thoughts and ideas.

This is where "mental minimalism" comes in. When working on something, it is crucial to liberate the mind from any unnecessary, distracting thoughts. These are the thoughts that can be postponed or set aside for another moment - and so we should jump at that opportunity to clear valuable mental space. We must be more intentional and organized in our thinking, just as we are (or at least, try to!) in other areas of our life - tackling one problem at a time rather than juggling various issues and thus ending up overwhelmed and unable to solve anything whatsoever.

Overthinking is also dangerous for our relationships because it implies the inability or refusal to trust other people entirely and to enjoy the moment without unnecessary paranoia. In both cases, excessive thinking and rumination lead to anxiety, frustration, and even invented problems - and so, the focus is lost from the real problems or goals we face.

Developing a Mental Framework thinking and first principles thinking

One example of "intelligent thinking" in this way is the one explained by Elon Musk about the first principles or about mental framework thinking. So... what on earth is mental framework thinking?

Think of how most companies - not unlike most minds - are largely disorganized and chaotic. Meetings (like your own internal monologues) seem endless and often have no obvious purpose. Initiatives tend to be loosely organized, following protocols and processes (your own habit loops) that follow no real logic.

However, "framework thinkers" are able to bring much-needed clarity to their thoughts. Effective frameworks, whether in the workplace or in your own mind, work by drowning out any background noise instead of focusing on the issues and ideas that truly matter. Framework

thinkers make more progress and strive for faster and easier solutions. They aren't caught up in the madness.
Here's the thing: there are rarely perfect answers in life, as nothing is black and white; this is why the ability to make faster decisions can often mean the all-important difference between success and failure. As you become someone who establishes frameworks effectively in your own thought processes, you become your own voice of reason in the chaos of your mind.

Mental Minimalism

Decluttering your mind.

So you may have heard of minimalism. This "less is more" movement taking the otherwise materialistic and consumerism world by the storm may not be everyone's cup of tea, but the philosophy behind it certainly lends some food for thought.

Mental minimalism, unlike regular minimalism, has no particular focus on material possessions - rather - it's our mental clutter that needs shedding. The concept asserts that keeping your mind in some sort of order will lead to a more intentional, focused mindset that is both wholesome and gratifying. Mental minimalism is about leaving behind the things that make us stressed and worried – they aren't doing you any favors so let them go. Easier said than done, I know. After giving up on the non-essential or destructive things on your mind, you carve out more time to simply be. To allow yourself to live in the moment. To take in the sensory buffet around you and remember that you are not just these rapid-fire thoughts (more on that later!). Simply put, it is about having less on your mind, but being more.

Downsizing our thoughts right down to the essential means we have to prioritize. This means that boundaries need to be established in order for any of this to work. For instance, if you reply to work emails late at night or at the weekend regularly, your colleagues will expect you to be available at those hours. Or, if you never decline an invitation to go out with friends, even if you're really not up to it and are simply doing it to please them, then they will assume that you always enjoy it, and will always be willing to give them your time and energy. What am I getting at? If we don't set boundaries for ourselves, other people will simply set them for us!

We can't do everything. We can't always say yes, always be there, or always show up. If we want to create time and space for ourselves and free up some precious mental energy, then we have to make room for it. This most likely means saying no sometimes – prioritizing your own mental health or even your own responsibilities over what others want from you. This isn't being selfish - it's being self-compassionate!

Organizing your mind at work

Healthy planning and balancing productivity with rest.

Quit the multitasking

Here's the thing about focus: despite what many will tell you, you can only focus on one thing at a time. Sure, many will jump between things - focus on one thing for one hour then another thing the next - but to be truly focused, we can only have that one thing on our mind. By incorporating mental minimalism as explained earlier, you are limiting the unnecessary distractions - tossing them out like work-out or unwanted clothes - so that you can see the capsule wardrobe of good quality, desirable pieces that you have left. You may have just three outfits left; you may have fifteen. The important thing is that you have a manageable number for you, enabling you to clearly see what you have to deal with every time you open the closet - then choose one (and only one!) outfit to wear at a time.

To-do lists are your friend

Your brain, while a biological miracle, still has to work with limited resources. Keeping a concise list of priority tasks each day that need to be accomplished is a great way to be more efficient. If you have a huge pile of tasks before you, it's easy to become overwhelmed, disheartened, or start ruminating about how you'll never get anything done, what will happen then, how terrible everything will be, et cetera… before you realize that if you actually got down to task number one, then in the time you spent overthinking everything, you could have already ticked something off the list!

On top of that, the human brain just loves written lists. They tap into our brain's intrinsic method of organizing itself and processing information. Furthermore, lists are categorical, which coincides with the brain's preference for memorizing things. And if nothing else, seeing the tasks you need to do separated into manageable bitesize chunks is great for your morale, and reminds you that when broken up into steps, you are more than capable of achieving what you need to.

Learn to disconnect

Modern society is obsessed with technology. After all, it is becoming increasingly harder to live without it – whether it's for pleasure or for work; and whether it's our smartphones or the fact that most jobs now have us chained to our desktops for most of the day. Many mental health experts propose that technology addiction – as in, a chemical and psychological dependence on the stuff – is a reality for millions of people.

This relentless overload of information and screen time is far from healthy, and we all know it but often choose to ignore it. The brain must have the chance to reflect, refresh and re-energize. A constant stream of incoming data is harmful - perhaps even more than we already realize - as it goes against the natural makeup and functioning of the human brain. This is especially apparent in the evening, as many of us have replaced our healthy bedtime reading rituals for endless scrolling of our social media news feeds until the early hours - not only overstimulating the brain making it even harder to shut down for sleep, but the blue light behind the screen actually inhibits the production of the sleep hormone, melatonin, as our primitive brains read this as sunlight - meaning we are not only frying our brains but not even allowing them the medicine of good quality sleep.

Do you know how your smartphone or computer overheats and crashes from time-to-time when it's been running for too long? The same concept applies to our brains. Sometimes they just need to be turned off for a little while before we restart them.

Take enough breaks

So we've established like any other advanced machine, your brain still has limited energy supplies at any one time. As such, we can't expect it always to work at full capacity. We wouldn't expect this of any computer - and yet we inflict this expectation on ourselves - when not only do we have the same limited energy issue, but also other complications like emotions and willpower thrown into the mix! The brain is similar to a machine in this sense: the more information that is processed, the more energy is consumed. And so, by constantly processing information - which could be studying for an exam, but it could also be simply talking to someone, or yes - overthinking while all by yourself.

These may not seem like particularly tiring tasks, but your brain begs to differ. You know that sound your computer makes (at least, if it is as old as mine is) and it makes that whirring sound? You can almost feel its discomfort. This is when you get that slightly guilty feeling - maybe you downloaded too many things or clicked a few too many times, and it got overloaded. Well, maybe extend this concern for the most valuable computer you'll ever own - the one between your ears!

Simply put, you can't expect to fire off thoughts for hours and maintain the same efficiency level. And so, breaks are absolutely fundamental for your brain.

Use a calendar

According to neuroscientists, keeping a calendar or schedule is an unbeatable method for externalizing your memories, thus allowing you to free up space in your brain. If you can make a quick note of where you need to be and when, then why use up precious brain space to hold onto this piece of information, cluttering other items that are perhaps more necessary to be uploaded onto your mental harddrive?.

Whether you prefer to download an app, use Outlook, or just get a good old-fashioned "flip" calendar like the one your mother probably adorns on her fridge (hey, she knows what she's doing) - habitually using and referring a calendar is a hugely underrated way to make your life become much easier and less stressful.

Get enough good-quality sleep

It's strange to think that until the 1950s, sleep was a largely misunderstood phenomenon. We just knew that at night, we eventually get tired and fall asleep until the morning. Today, however, scientists know that sleep is a crucial part of maintaining healthy brain function. When we don't get enough sleep, numerous problems arise: from concentration to hand-eye coordination, to memory loss and mood instability. I'm sure we've all been there at some point and can vouch for these claims personally…

Scientists generally agree that a minimum of seven hours of sleep is necessary for adults. But it's not only the quantity but also the quality that you need to be aware of. For many of us, we can just tell from waking up whether we had what we call "a good night's sleep" or not… Sleep gives a chance for your brain to reorder itself. Temporarily free from the burden of your constant daytime demands and thought processes – it begins the night shift. Essentially, it sifts through the thoughts you had that day – the jury is still out when it comes to the precise workings of the mind during slumber – it's mysterious in that way – but what we do know is that it doesn't stop. Far from it – MRI scans have proven that the brain is hard at work even when your consciousness switches off. And science also tells us that our brain function deteriorates dramatically the longer we go sleep-deprived – so let's do it a favor and just let it do its thing, okay?

Never Stop Learning

Here's another thing that neuroscience has discovered about our brains: it continues to reshape itself throughout life - even throughout adulthood. It was once believed that the brain stopped developing after adolescence or young adulthood. However, we now know that our brains actually continue to change over the course of your entire lifetime - depending, of course, on how we nourish it.

When you learn something new - whatever it is - your brain creates new connections. It could be how to speak a new language, or simply a new recipe. But over time of practicing this new skill, reinforcing the new connections we built, these new connections gradually work to change the overall structure of this particular part of your brain. Scientists call this phenomenon "neuroplasticity". The significance of its discovery tells us more about our capacity for learning and how to heal traumatic injuries and neurological diseases.

We really underestimated our brains for some time, but if we feed them well (with sleep, rest, and learning), then they truly blossom.

How overthinking ruins relationships

Avoid thinking your problems into existence

Overthinking and the mental junk accumulated, as a result, can damage your relationship more than you can probably even imagine. Relationships of any kind are complicated enough as they are. After all, humans are complicated - and for two to get along without too much fuss and while establishing boundaries, trust, and maybe, even love and mutual understanding - can be a complete minefield especially, if at least one party is an overthinker, with limited mental clarity thanks to their piles of mental junk not letting them see straight. Of course, I am not encouraging you to simply wash your hands of all of life's causes for concern or preoccupation; To deny any real issues your relationship may have, for example. However, incessant worrying will only do more harm than good - not actually solving your problems while giving you even more to worry about as your overworked brain causes additional trouble!

In one study, 40 different couples completed questionnaires to determine their overall relationship satisfaction. The catch? Half of the couples were asked to analyze the relationship before completing the questionnaire. They had to 'list all the reasons why your relationship with your dating partner is going the way it is, and to take time to analyze why it is good or bad.' Then, immediately after analyzing their relationships in this straight-to-the-point fashion, they completed the questionnaire. Meanwhile, the control group simply answered the satisfaction questionnaire without this step of first analyzing their relationship.

All couples in both groups were then contacted between four and eight months later to determine whether they were still together. And do you know what happened? The couples in the control group (who skipped the analysis part) demonstrated a strong correlation between how satisfied they claimed to be in the questionnaire, and whether or not they separated when contacted several months later. In other words, self-reported happier couples were more likely to have stayed together. Predictable so far.

However, for the couples who were asked to analyze their relationships in detail before answering the questionnaire about relationship satisfaction, there was almost no correlation between how happy they reported being, and whether or not they went their separate ways. Essentially, the way they felt about their relationships after this rigorous analysis was completely unrelated to whether or not they ended up staying together. This is because analyzing their relationship beforehand had actually created confusion just in time for the questionnaire that followed - they may have overthought their relationship to the point that they had fabricated problems that then seeped into their questionnaire answers. Essentially, the pre-analysis had left participants scrambled and led to the questionnaire being a much less accurate measurement for compatibility.

What can we determine from this? Quite simply, overthinking - though you may think since it suggests thinking a lot, it may pay off in some way - actually reduces mental clarity.

So why does over-analysis often only lead to more confusion in this way? One possible reason is that it causes us to believe that we have a deeper insight than we actually do - and that we must pay more attention to these alleged insights rather than our actual behavior. Therefore, rather than only taking how you and your partner interact with each other as an indicator of whether or not your relationship will last, you unwittingly fabricate thoughts and theories that actually distance you away from the facts.

On top of that, many of our behaviors and preferences are actually unconscious. As a result, we don't even know the true sources of our feelings. All we know is that we feel them and then come up with reasoning - yet the problem is it is often difficult to assess the validity of our own emotions... And so, we try to make sense of it all by making up rational explanations concerning the other person involved. They must be wrong, or irrational, not me—but these explanations are not accurate. Our emotions are especially complex and often irrational. Consequently, attempting to apply rational tactics to determine why we feel a certain way can create even more confusion about our emotional state.

Additionally, we are also pretty bad when it comes to predicting our emotional reactions to future events. We typically overestimate the strength and duration of future emotional responses, whether positive and negative. We overthink how things will feel, exaggerating them in the process. You will most likely have noticed it - when the anticipation of something turns out to be more intense than the emotions you feel when the moment you've been waiting for actually comes. This also applies to our relationships, as we tend to overestimate how happy we will be to enter into a relationship with someone, or even how unhappy we will be following a breakup. This effect seems to be particularly driven by our tendency to imagine the extremes in our overthinking. We blow things way out of proportion in our minds. This habitual overestimation of our future emotional responses occurs because when we think towards a potential future event, we forget that it wouldn't exist in isolation. In other words, your relationship may end, but you'll still have your job, routine, friends, and other things that bring joy, purpose, or satisfaction to your life. Furthermore, we tend to underestimate our future selves' emotional resilience: we can actually deal with a lot more than we tend to give ourselves credit for.

So, how can you give a relationship the best possible chance at success? Firstly, don't overthink or over-analyze it: nothing is perfect, and if you magnify every minute doubt or perceived flaw, you will never find happiness. Secondly, when assessing the potential impact of the break-up, think more broadly about how your future would look - with all the rest of your current life intact. You may still feel grief and a degree of sadness, of course. But your life is more than your relationship, and your resilience is a lot stronger than you think it is.

The Bottom Line: Time For a Mental Clear-Out!

Before the age of 50, Elon Musk has now innovated and built three ground-breaking multi-billion dollar companies in completely different fields. At first glance, you would be forgiven for linking his rapid success, his proven ability to solve seemingly unsolvable problems, and his creativity to his unbreakable work ethic. No doubt, work ethic plays an important role in succeeding and reaching the heights of your potential — but there's more to it than that. Look around - or maybe in the mirror: there are unfailingly dedicated and hardworking people who can currently not even dream of such achievement. And for most of us, we never will. What then, you may ask, is the missing jigsaw piece for the vast majority of us?

Some of the most world-changing and incredible minds of all time to date — from Aristotle, to Marie Curie, to Thomas Edison— you could say, incorporate a missing link to marry together their curiosity and enthusiasm for learning, complex problem-solving and creativity. This missing link actually has relatively little to do with how hard they work; rather, it's about how they think.

The most successful people - however diverse - tend to have one major thing in common: the practice of actively questioning every assumption they possess - and not taking anything a given. You may think you 'know' about a given problem or scenario — just as people throughout history thought they "knew" that the world was flat or that children cannot feel pain... Quitting overthinking doesn't mean quitting curiosity, questioning or reason. Usually, when we're faced with complex problems, we aim to tackle it like we imagine as everybody else would, or how we deem is the normal response. "First-principles thinking" is a powerful way to help you break free from this limiting herd mentality; think outside the box and innovate new solutions to familiar problems. But of course, to hope for such clarity and creativity - we must throw out all the mental junk first!

Chapter 4
I'm not my thoughts, I'm what I do

For many of my overthinking clients, it's hard to separate this habit from their personality. This means that you actually cease to see overthinking as a habit that can be stopped, but you actually view it as an integral part of your personality. You perhaps cannot imagine a version of yourself that doesn't excessively ruminate over things in this way. Once this mindset is in place, the overthinking habit becomes worryingly fixes it in place. But not because the client is correct in thinking in this way! Rather, as soon as we see something as "just how it is" or "simply the way I am," it becomes a sort of self-fulfilling prophecy where the individual overthinks about how they overthink, and so, the cycle continues. If you don't believe you can be helped, then not much can be done.

However, once you see overthinking and rumination as the bad habit that it is, to which anyone is susceptible, then you realise that you can overcome it and still be you - just a mentally healthier and less anxious version.

Now for some advice on the correct habits to have if you want to try to think less, worry less, and be more productive in life. I want to talk about the importance of a pre-established routine so that we don't have to waste time and go crazy thinking about what to do every day because everything will already be decided at the beginning.

Changing your habits

The importance of daily routine and physical health.

Your Overthinking Isn't Who You Are

The trouble is, rumination gives you a warped, pessimistic perspective on yourself and the way your life is panning out. Overthinking also drains your mental resources, which can interfere with your judgment and ability to problem-solve. As a result, you end up caught in a tangle of self-destructive or self-flagellating thoughts, and yet no insight or clarity is gained. Instead, rumination only makes you feel worse about whatever is on your mind.

Introverts, especially, need quiet time for self-reflection and introspection, because they are often more sensitive to everything around them, they crave downtime, without distraction or interruption from the outside world, to process the stuff of the day—the interactions, their reactions to them, and simply to think their thoughts. Introspection is about self-growth, looking inward in order to learn from the challenges we're facing.

It is essential to be in tune with your own physical and mental state in order to understand why you are overthinking and how you can stop it. Here are some concrete tips on how to get there:

The Importance of Sleep

Overthinking at night is largely down to the brain processing what has happened to us during the day. Since our days now present us with such a lot of stimuli - we're communicating more and taking in and processing more information - we don't allow for gaps in order to process our thoughts during the daytime.

We don't have the time and space during the day to process what's happened and to evaluate and make sense of it. Sometimes the only opportunity we get to do this is when we're in bed, trying to get some precious sleep. A lot of clients tell me that as soon as their head hits the pillow and they close their eyes, all their niggling thoughts start coming out of the shadows – suddenly remembering all the things that may have been lying dormant in the back of their mind throughout the day.

On top of that, this is a vicious cycle of rumination and insomnia, as night-time rumination hinders sleep while lack of sleep actually increases stress levels, and thus your tendency to be anxious and overthink things throughout your day. So overall, we should all be prioritizing sleep. Adults should be getting at least seven or eight hours a night. The importance of our sleeping habits regarding our mental clarity and overall well-being cannot be underestimated. After all, we spend around a third of our lives sleeping, which should be seen as the catalyst for making the other two thirds successful, rewarding and energized. We cannot hope to perform our best or even think with clarity when our perception is clouded by the physical and mental exhaustion inflicted by sleep deprivation.

"Eat the frog first"

Here's a great habit that can change your life for the better: strive always to do your worst task first thing in the morning. Every single day, you've got one major to-do that you know should be your top priority - but despite this, it can often be the most difficult one to start. On top of that, when you've got the whole day ahead of you, it's easy to just put things off "until later" - after that meeting, or after running that errand. You may think since you are not a "morning person", or you feel so tired and unmotivated first thing in the morning, you feel the need to ease yourself in by starting with easier tasks, and putting off whatever you may be dreading to the afternoon.

However, this only gives you the opportunity to ruminate over this less appealing item on your to-do list for the whole day. And worse still - if you keep telling yourself "not yet" or "I'll come back to it later," - the chances are, you will end up eventually telling yourself "not today" and "I'll deal with this tomorrow." So that's a whole day wasted while you put off this task, only to then repeat this same twisted routine the very next day. We all know this isn't logical, and yet we kid ourselves into thinking we are being kind to ourselves by putting ourselves through this mental torture and willpower gymnastics. It would have been a lot kinder to rip off the bandaid or swallow the pill as soon as we could - to save ourselves the burden!

By "worst" task, this could either be the hardest, or it could even be the most important thing on your agenda, which is making you feel uneasy for whatever reason. Whatever it is that you are procrastinating, as touched upon earlier, our anticipation of negative feelings is often completely exaggerated. In other words, most often, whatever we are dreading most likely isn't so bad once we bite the bullet. So at the risk of parroting a well-known sportswear brand, just do it; before you can do anything else to distract yourself, before you have time to think about it too much.

Mark Twain notoriously called this strategy "eating your frog." He declared that if the first thing you do each morning is "eat a live frog," then you can go through the rest of the day comforted in the knowledge that the worst is already behind you. Your own "frog" is the task you are most dreading. By jumping in and crossing this off straight away, the rest of your day will seem easier and more manageable.

First thing in the morning your mind is clear, the world is only just waking up, and so your attention likely hasn't yet been pulled into six different directions. This is your one opportunity to prioritize the thing that matters to you most before other responsibilities and distractions start to pile up. And, by ticking off something important on your to-do list before anything else, you get both the required momentum and a sense of achievement - all before 10 am!

And so, set yourself up to eat your frog tomorrow morning last thing before you call it a day tonight. Identify tomorrow's frog - and write it down on a post-it or notepad that you'll see when you return to your desk in the morning. If you can, gather together whatever materials you'll need to get it done and have that out, too, so that all you'll have to do tomorrow is get your nose stuck in it. Getting things done efficiently and without unnecessary fuss and overthinking is a great habit to instill, and if you start each day by accomplishing something important, you'll feel like a small weight has lifted before you're even in the thick of your day. This little boost you will get will only spur you on to achieve more and more, causing your productivity to snowball.

Leverage Your Unique Energy Levels

The key to stepping out of this overthinking mode is focusing on increasing your productivity. Keeping your mind busy with more tangible tasks is a surefire way to keep any niggling doubts and insecurities threatening your inner peace at bay. And this kind of sustainable productivity, unshaken by the storms brewing in your head, can be achieved by leveraging your own natural energy levels. This may sound pretty abstract, but seizing the ebbs and flows of your natural energy levels is about understanding yourself; observing and acknowledging the natural patterns and rhythm of your body's energy flow - both the surges and the dips - and thus harnessing your energy peaks when they occur.

Your ultradian rhythms are your body's natural cycles of energy and are key to maintaining motivation and stamina. Just like the tides, sometimes your energy levels are more powerful and gushing, and sometimes they temporarily recede. It's all-natural and nothing to try to fix or correct, but to embrace.

Many people senselessly try to push through a task, whipping their body and mind into submission, even when they are mentally exhausted and haven't got any more creative input to offer. This is a highly damaging and counterproductive – you can't pour from an empty cup, after all. Or pour from an empty cup. We can only be productive when our reserves are replenished - that means getting enough sleep, food, and water - but it also means having sufficient mental and emotional breaks too. Or choosing to rest or carry out a more basic task when you naturally have lower energy levels, leaving your most challenging tasks to when you feel mentally capable. Understanding your own energy cycles and taking advantage of your energy bursts while acknowledging when your energy is at a natural low. Thus, incorporating some deliberate rest will ultimately make you more productive - and of course, less stressed.

Getting through an entire workday while maximizing your productivity requires breaks throughout the day to account for these ebbs and flows. If you refuse to take adequate breaks, then you will only make more errors, experience more stress and fatigue, and mess up your immune, nervous, and endocrine (hormone) systems. So this is serious stuff!

These frequent breaks don't have to be long or elaborate. Something as quick and simple as taking a quick stroll in a nearby park, or taking a few minutes to stretch or meditate could be just the step back you need to then return to your task feeling brimming with motivation and ideas again. Whatever type of break you choose, be disciplined about it. During this period of mental rest, try not to let thoughts about your tasks creep into your consciousness - you'll have plenty of time for that later! But you will only reap the benefits of your break if you allow yourself to truly disconnect from your worries and responsibilities. There's no skipping this important step if you want to get some quality work done at all today. It's like refueling your creativity - don't expect to just have fresh ideas on tap at all hours if you don't even stop to recharge!

Changing your environment

Giving your mind a break! It will thank you.
It is said while Albert Einstein was in the process of formulating his groundbreaking theory of relativity, he

achieved his greatest lightbulb-moment breakthrough while taking a short break from working to relax by a fire and let his mind rest.

Not only does this support the argument that breaks are a help and not a hindrance to productivity, but also that changes in environment can be just what you need to encourage new ways of thinking. Sometimes, we remain at our desks and push ourselves until we can't give anymore - but it's not until we finally give in and take a walk, or even just go for a bathroom break or get up to open a window, that the answer we've been racking our brain for comes to us. Why does this happen? Because our brains get quickly bored. When we focus on one thing for too long, it becomes less and less clear. Eventually, we lose focus of the task - but this only tends to make us even more frustrated with ourselves - and so we overthink, we push too hard, and thus, the vicious cycle continues...

If you find yourself overthinking, or struggling to think straight and achieve focus, simply change your environment. Go to a coffee shop, take a quick walk in a park or, simply shift your attention on another task for a while. You could give the computer a rest and switch to pencil and paper. Or simply stop thinking about the problem for a moment, and just allow yourself to daydream. They say that many of our most creative thoughts come to us while in the shower. Well, this is why. Allowing ourselves to temporarily move away from our daily responsibilities and letting our minds wander is often when we inadvertently stumble upon the jackpot. A kettle watched never boils!

Focus on one single task

As mentioned in the last chapter, multitasking is a lie. We may be able to go back and forth between tasks, but this is usually no help, and only further scrambles our thoughts and stresses us out even more.

Richoteting between different tasks or projects may seem to keep things exciting, or even make you believe you are being more productive and efficient by tackling more than one thing at once. However, in truth, this habit doesn't do you or your productivity any favors. Instead, although focusing on just one task for a long period of time may be difficult - especially with smartphones by our sides most of the time - practicing "single-tasking," as in, taking your tasks one at a time and devoting your attention fully to each one until it is complete, can help to rebuild your focus and attention span and keep any overthinking and procrastination at bay.

According to a Harvard study carried out in 2010, we spend 46.9% of our time thinking about something other than what we're actually doing in that given moment. And this habitual mental time-travel prevents us from enjoying the present, having a great impact on both our ability to relax, and to feel contented.

Concentrating solely on just one task for a long duration of time can be testing, especially with smartphones in our hand and our eyes fixated on a screen of some sort for most of our waking hours. However, practicing "single-tasking" can help to rebuild both your capacity to your focus, and attention span overall. It's less mentally overwhelming and more natural for your mind to focus on one thing at a time, and you're more likely to tap into your flow state, which Mihaly Csikszentmihalyi describes as the 'secret to happiness.'

Therefore, you can also use this as a mind trick to avoid incessant rumination. Next time you are struggling with anxious, racing thoughts, try singling out one particular task - no matter how seemingly trivial in the scheme of things - such as tidying your workspace or doing your laundry. This can not only serve as a great distraction from your racing mind, as it forces you to fill your consciousness with the straightforward task at hand, but it also chips away at the pile of things at the back of your mind you feel you need to do. Once the simple stuff is out of the way, it is as though you clear mental space to tackle the bigger things on your mind.

The Importance of Action (Step by Step)

Often, when we discuss goals – whether it's to make more money, to lose weight, or to build a business – we talk about the bigger actions. I often sing the praises of taking concrete action to see results myself.

However, although this leap into action is the crux of short-term achievements, it is consistency that will set you up for long-term success. Here is the problem: Every action cis presented with resistance. We may want to start that business but we may have to give up the security of our job. We may want to live a healthier life, but our temptations present a real psychological resistance. We may want to improve our mental health and well-being, and yet our stubborn thoughts continue to race around our minds, threatening to sabotage any such goals...

Even by just taking that first small step action, we need to break through the resistance of our procrastination, our lack of self-confidence or self-efficacy, or the resistance of that critical voice in the back of our minds telling us our goals are ridiculous. To overcome our personal resistances, we need copious amounts of mental energy. And as already discussed, our level of mental energy is not constant - we have peaks and troughs even throughout a single day. Sometimes we feel like the world is our oyster, and other times we feel completely defeated.

Set your own standards; Be your own motivator

This is a key reason why people depend heavily on external motivation. That is: allowing the promise of others' praise, or the fear of their disapproval spur you forward, rather than allowing your own inner voice to keep you moving. We all know that it's best to be our own motivators - but sometimes we don't feel like this is enough - even though this is the only sustainable option. External motivators can be fickle - people's reactions can be unpredictable, and you may become enslaved by the worry of what others think about you - whether it's your boss, your partner, or your mother! We all are striving to please someone else through our actions - but really, we should be striving to please ourselves above all else. This way, we can know for sure if we made ourselves proud. We aren't always waiting to see what someone else thinks.

This external dependence is why people often start with something big and always slip off after sometimes—for instance, going from never working out to starting to do so for 3 hours a day. Or forcing yourself to write 10,000 on your first day trying to write the novel you've always dreamed of writing. We pick these goals out of thin air - maybe because that's what your friend or your colleague, or someone you saw on Instagram is doing... But our goals need to be tailored to our own abilities, needs, and aspirations!

And what tends to happen in these kinds of copy-cat scenarios? The first day or two is such a stretch, and so unnatural for our usual routine, that we fail to produce enough mental energy to resist the temptation to give up altogether. We could have tried just a 3 hours working out spread over a week, to begin with, or only writing the first 1000 words in your first day of writing - this would have been more sustainable, would have given you the little high needed to maintain your motivation levels, and would have been the first small steps into a huge achievement. It seems like a no-brainer, and yet many of us feel so motivated at the beginning that we break off more than we can chew, and then end up packing it in altogether.

The Bottom Line: You're not your thoughts, you're what you do

The more we think about thoughts, the more we think about how bizarre it is to think. To overthink. To think about how you wished you didn't overthink. And to then realize you're overthinking it.

The thing about thoughts is that they emerge from your consciousness inadvertently, to then slip away as easily as they appear to make room for the next one. This is how our brain has functioned from as long as we have been able to think. We can't imagine not thinking because even that requires thinking. And so, this is so natural to us, we don't even… think about it.

To pin your identity to your thoughts is misleading since they come about in an uncontrollable way. This is why so many struggle with intrusive thoughts - when unwanted thoughts or compulsions repeatedly pop up in one's mind, and they feel completely unable to overcome them or stop them from entering their consciousness. Many believe that these bad thoughts make them a bad person, or that thinking certain things makes them crazy. But we cannot control what pops into our mind! In fact, the more we worry about something popping into our mind, the more it pops up.

I guess what I'm getting at is that the more we think about something, the longer it lingers in your mind. So if we are thinking about unpleasant things, or things we wished we didn't think about so much, then they will inevitably only outstay their welcome even longer. It's easier said than done to simply stop thinking about something. The more we try, the more impossible it becomes. But by using techniques to break out of this overthinking cycle altogether, we can not only free ourselves from this prison of rumination, freeing up mental space and energy for more worthwhile, pleasant and productive matters, but we also learn that we are not our thoughts, but rather our actions.

As author Eckhart Tolle states:

"Be present as the watcher of your mind — of your thoughts and emotions as well as your reactions in various situations. Be at least as interested in your reactions as in the situation or person that causes you to react."

To overthink and ruminate about disempowering thoughts only reinforces them in your mind. And so, to overcome the burden of overthinking, pay attention to your thoughts by being mindful of your mental landscape - what could be triggering it in your environment or your emotional state - and intercept them before they get the chance to wreak havoc. You may not be able to control your thoughts - but you can control how you react to them!

Chapter 5

Perfectionism vs excellence

We are often taught that if we want to get results, we have to strive for perfection: perfect skills, perfect self-discipline, and perfect actions. But this is unrealistic and a harmful expectation to impose on ourselves. Whether you are a perfectionist with your work, your health and fitness level, your relationship, your looks, or any other way that you rank your success in your life - it only sets us up for a life of sweating the small stuff, overthinking ourselves into oblivion, and sabotaging our own satisfaction and even - ironically - our success.

And yet, despite the growing body of research revealing that perfectionism puts you at a greater risk of anxiety, depression, and even heart problems, many of us still believe perfectionism is a positive attribute. Sometimes, we get trapped in a vicious cycle of toxic perfectionism, where we set ourselves a target so challenging to reach that it is unrealistic, and yet the perfectionist within pushes you to the absolute mental, physical, and emotional limit in order to give all you have in the name of this ill-founded goal. The result? We wind up working ourselves to the bone, and yet still believing ourselves to have "underachieved."

We must learn that sometimes imperfection is often natural, expected, and nothing to be afraid of. For instance, you may have gotten one question in an exam wrong, but still excelled overall. Is this reason to berate yourself? Of course not! Be glad that you excelled, and learn from that one mistake you made. This is why we must aim for excellence rather than perfection. To strive for overall success and happiness - and not a life or career absolutely free from mistakes or obstacles.

Perfectionism is ultimately a self-defeating way to live your life. It is built on the painful irony: that making mistakes - as well as admitting them and allowing yourself to move past them - is a necessary part of growing up and being a human being in this world. With every mistake, you learn something about how to do better next time - whether it regards your career, your relationships, or your life overall. By avoiding mistakes at all costs, you are essentially wrapping yourself up in cotton wool to avoid all potential risk - and this is actually hindering your personal growth and self-development by not allowing yourself to aim high, regardless of the obstacles you will inevitably face along the way.

Perfectionism has also been linked to a whole host of health issues, such as depression, anxiety, self-harm, eating disorders, obsessive-compulsive disorder (OCD), insomnia, heart problems, chronic headaches, and - most tragically of all, early mortality and suicide. And so I must reiterate, no one should ever try or even want to be perfect. Life is so much more than that!

Where does perfectionism come from?

Perfectionism is a result of social conditioning, established in mind from childhood. Parents, teachers, and other adults in your early life can easily, and perhaps unwittingly, imprint this attitude that anything less than perfection is failure. Just think back to how you were likely graded at school. Or how you may have tried to impress your teachers or parents by getting everything right. Of course, some children succumb to this more than others, but for many - perfectionist or not - we grow up believing that there's a right way and a wrong way, and that every failure tarnishes our self-worth somehow. Exactly what perfection entails is often nebulous and ends up being what the adult says it is.

Of course, it wasn't your parents' or your teacher's fault - this is simply how society currently functions - and how they will have been conditioned too. We all go through life believing success to be this rigid binary that we either master or miss altogether.

This perhaps explains why the crux of perfectionism is "external locus of control," which simply means that someone seeks validation – which in this case is the confirmation of perfection – from outside of oneself. Even if someone holds their own standard of perfection, this standard stems from the adults around them while growing up. It is not usually a standard that was consciously, intelligently, and maturely chosen after some level of deliberate thought.

Perfectionism, by definition, suggests a standard both unrealistic and also based on an external measure. Therefore, the first step to overcome perfectionism is the recognition that these standards are external; They aren't based on your own values and ideals but on someone else's that have somehow been instilled in you. Think about it: a lot of what we do – consciously or not – is to impress others. If you focus on what you really want and expect instead, you can save yourself a lot of unnecessary pressure, and have more clarity about what success looks like to you.

For instance, was it your parents who instilled the idea in you that owning a detached property and being married with two kids before 35 is what success looks like? Was it your social circle that made you believe that success means working in a high-rise office building in the inner-city sending emails all day? Or, maybe it's the online content you consume that makes you see success as having a toned physique, or traveling the whole world before you "settle down"?

Whatever you may have been led to believe success must look like for you, it's best to be your own author - to come up with your own ideals and dreams, rather than basing them on other's standards. This alignment between your true ambitions and your actions is the closest anyone can get to perfection! And since this looks so different to every individual, the whole concept of perfection becomes obsolete anyway...

Of course, even your own internal standards can be highly unrealistic, likely still influenced at least somewhat by your past and who you spend your time with. Just remember that constantly striving to be "the best" causes increased stress and anxiety - only reducing your chances of performing well. By adopting a more casual approach, you inflict less tension and pressure on yourself, and your performance will likely improve.

Why we are so Obsessed with Perfection

And so, culturally, we still often regard perfectionism as a positive. Even saying you have perfectionistic tendencies is regarded as a coy form of self-promotion or "humble brag." So much so that it's practically become the stock answer to the fateful "What's your greatest weakness?" job interview question.

And admittedly, some researchers propose that there is an adaptive – or 'healthy' – form of perfectionism, characterized by setting high standards for yourself, self-motivation and self-discipline. However, there is also a maladaptive, 'unhealthy' version – when your best just never seems to be good enough, and not meeting goals frustrates you to the point that you berate yourself or even end up loathing or harming yourself. And while research shows that these more maladaptive and self-destructive perfectionist attributes may make you more susceptible to chronic anxiety and depression, other studies show that 'adaptive' perfectionist traits like striving for achievement and pushing yourself to accomplish your goals have no effect at all, or may even protect you from such mental problems by giving you a sense of purpose and direction.

Doing the right thing vs. doing the things right

Strive for Excellence, Not Perfection

So how can you switch from a perfectionist mindset to an excellent one?

Pursuers of excellence value themselves by who they are, and strive for the best - but when they fail, they pick themselves up, see the positives of the experience, and learn from their mistakes. Perfectionists, on the other hand, when they run into difficulty, become easily overwhelmed and often give up once a perfect outcome no-longer seems likely. Pursuers of excellence experience setbacks and temporary disappointment, of course, but they keep going anyway - viewing themselves as more than simply their past achievements. They focus on the present - what they can do now to make tomorrow better. Perfectionists obsess over past mistakes and ruminate over worries for tomorrow, so tend to overlook what they can do to be productive in the here and now.

Perfectionists feel they must always come out on top and be the best. Anything less, and they feel disappointed. However, pursuers of excellence don't compare their achievements to those of others in this way, recognizing that we each are on our own journey, and must only compare ourselves today with who we were yesterday. This goes to show why perfectionists hate criticism, and often cannot cope unless they receive nothing but praise, treating any commentary less than complete awe as evidence that they have failed. However, pursuers of excellence see criticism as a way to learn and are more open in general to others' opinions and ideas - as they are more adaptive and less blinkered to their own specific perspective and expectations.

Overall, perfectionists have to win or get things 100% right to maintain high self-esteem. Pursuers of excellence, however, can still feel good within themselves; however, a particular challenge or task turned out. They will always keep striving to do better next time - but remain content with where they're at right now.

And so, as you will now understand, there is a clear difference between being a perfectionist and excellent. Having said that, what would you prefer to be? Later in the chapter, I will give you useful tips to put into practice to harness your unique kind of excellence.

Tactical Thinking versus Strategic Thinking

This "perfection" versus "excellence" paradigm is comparable to the concept of tactical versus strategic thinking. Tactical thinkers are those who tend to focus on "doing things right," whereas strategic thinkers are more concerned with "doing the right things" the way they perceive it. As you can imagine - like the perfectionist, the tactical thinker sees tasks as a list of rules to be followed. There's no room for flexibility, adaption, or human error is you're a perfectionist tactical-thinking person! It might sound like these are the people who have it together - but life cannot be lived in this way! And even the most high-level work cannot be carried out in this way. It's narrow-minded, unsustainable, and glosses over the fact that we are human - and both adaptation and some mistakes here and there are part and parcel of how we do things.

Doing the right things by the book involves doing things obediently and efficiently. However, this may not be enough; the most successful people aren't those who spend their lives following rules and living their every decision by some pre-decided guidelines set out by someone else. No, a leader is someone who uses their own intellect and capacities to decide to do the most appropriate according to the specific situation. This is called being strategic. If you want to be innovative and do something that others have not yet done, then being a perfectionist, or merely a tactical thinker, will not be enough.

The Link Between Anxiety and Perfectionism

Lower your standards; increase your quality of life.

As discussed earlier, our anxiety - that heart-racing, nausea-inducing panic or dread we feel - sometimes just by thinking alone - is a result of our age-old fight-or flight stress response. This neurophysiological reaction is what jerks us into gear and prepares us for what our bodies believe is a life-or-death situation - an attack, or a fight. As also discussed, this biological hype-up we may feel every time we think of all the work we have to get done tomorrow, or about giving that presentation next week serves us no purpose today other than to make sure we get no sleep, lose our appetite, and have basically every bodily function - from our circulation right down to our reproductive system - suffer tremendously as a result.

It perhaps comes as no shock, then, that perfectionism alone can fuel this fire of anxiety. This obsession with getting things a certain way, never being happy with what you have and always striving for bigger, better, more - will only harm you both mentally and physically in the long run. Yes - this is a perfectionists nightmare - as the more you strive for perfection, the more imperfectly your body and mind can function...

So as you can perhaps now imagine, your perfectionism may well be fanning the flames of your anxiety and overthinking. However, through some careful practice and work on your self-awareness, you may be able to "loosen up" a little to get a better handle on your perfectionism - as well as the anxious and overthinking tendencies that often come with it! Here are some pointers on where to begin:

Overcome your negative thoughts: Perfectionism is often fueled by habitual negative thoughts. You can get past this way of thinking through techniques such as writing exercises and positive affirmations. Quieting your negative thoughts about perfectionism can also help you to remain realistic and self-forgiving about what you set out to accomplish.

Build your self-esteem: Perfectionism often has a harmful impact on your self-esteem. This is because if you tend to evaluate your own sense of self-worth according to the flawlessness of your performance, then your self-esteem is doomed to plummet as soon as these lofty expectations are not met. Combine this with the fact that a perfectionist's goals are often unrealistic in the first place, and you set yourself up for avoidable disappointment. Rather being so self-critical, channel this energy into elevating your self-esteem, however that may look for you. For example, allowing yourself to rest and recharge (including your mind!), focusing on your strengths and abilities rather than any weaknesses or perceived limitations, practicing self-care, and finding ways to support others who could use your help.

Limit stress: Perfectionist tendencies can be a fundamental contributor to your daily stress levels. Persistent stress can drain energy, increase your overthinking, and fuel any anxiety and depression you may be dealing with. So make every effort to release yourself from the stress over your irrational obsession with perfectionism by constantly reminding yourself that perfect isn't real, and things don't have to be 100% as you planned them in order for them to be excellent. Of course, some stress will often still remain. But you can better manage these other challenges in your life if things not being perfect isn't a cause!

How to be a perfect imperfectionist

How to be productive but stop chasing "perfect."

And so, those who strive for perfection may think they are simply being ambitious or determined, but they often only unwittingly deprive themselves of contentment and life satisfaction, no matter how much they end up achieving. So how can you get out of this claustrophobia-inducing mindset and loosen up a bit for your own good?

Be Kind to Yourself: Being kind to ourselves may be easy on some days - when we are on a temporary self-esteem high, or simply are having a good day. But then, suddenly, we make a mistake, or are made aware of a weakness or setback. Our inner voice becomes an inner critic, and we somehow forget all the things that we previously were proud of ourselves for. We abandon ourselves and look towards others for validation and comfort.

Self-kindness refers to acting in kind and understanding ways towards ourselves. For instance, showing forgiveness and understanding for the mistakes we make - just as we show (hopefully!) to those around us. Humanity is blessed with the recognition that everyone makes mistakes sometimes, and no one is exempt from weaknesses or occasional failures. Extensive research has shown the copious positive consequences of self-compassion for overall wellbeing - including greater life satisfaction, emotional intelligence, connections and relationships with others, wisdom, and happiness. Self-compassion is also associated with fewer instances of depression, anxiety, fear of failure, and of course - perfectionism.

Lower Your Standards: You might not like the sound of this one, but hear me out! One of the most toxic elements of perfectionism is the tendency to set unrealistic goals and standards. For instance, you may decide you want to finish writing your novel in two weeks, and then berate yourself when the time window you set for yourself passes, and you don't manage. Or you may decide that you need to get 100% in all of your exams in order to feel like you did yourself proud. But this is a near-impossible feat, even for the most intellectual and conscientious of students - and getting around 80-90% in each test may be more than enough, as well as a clear indication of your excellence. So why set unachievable standards that only serve to give you a sense of disappointment even when in reality, your achievements may be truly great. The simple belief that 'if I don't meet this particular standard, then I am a failure' is toxically perfectionistic. There is no allowance for a middle ground. No flexibility in terms of what could be deemed a successful outcome. It is either success or failure, and that's that. But this isn't how life works!

In fact, it's possible to be just 80% or 75% successful - even a 30% success does not equate to failure. You may not have ticked all the boxes this time - but some of them, you did. And next time you will tackle the rest. So snap out of the black-and-white way of thinking that makes you believe every outcome only has two options - good or bad, yes or no, pass or fail. Open yourself up to nuance and the scope for possibility multiplies. Suddenly, it's not all about winning or losing anymore. It's about how you succeed, and how you learn from the times when you don't. It's about striving for excellence in all that you do, part of which is the learning process that lies behind every mistake. In that sense, failure is little more than feedback. And we all need feedback in order to better ourselves!

Another common perfectionist mindset is that 'if I am not the absolute best, then I'm no good at all.' This toxically competitive mindset is based on the idea that perfect means first place - and anything less equates to failure. This black-and-white approach to your achievements is not only blinkered to the many possible outcomes other than "first" or "last" - or "perfect" and "imperfect" - but it is also far too heavily focused on external measures. Essentially, you are comparing your own success to others' rather than focusing on your own unique journey. Many of us find this attitude hard to shake off after a decade or two of an education system ingraining within us the idea of grades and rankings - making us obsessed with the details, and comparing ourselves to our peers. But out in the real world, it doesn't have to be this way!

So, how to overcome this lingering grade-A student attitude?

Set Time Limits: One thing that your perfectionist attitude will never be able to overcome, despite its best efforts, is time. By setting hard time limits for projects and sticking to them, you will force yourself to come to draw lines under your endeavors before they manage to send you spiraling into hyper-vigilant perfectionist mode. Preening and re-doing your work obsessively when it was most likely already great before you started overthinking it will do you no favors. If you are naturally a perfectionist, you likely drive yourself mad by oscillating between wanting to always be on time, and wanting everything to be perfect. But not every task you do can take up huge amounts of your time and energy. It simply isn't feasible.

Of course, there are tasks that call for more of your attention than others, but if you find yourself going over and over every projects or endeavor, to the point that your eyes are sore and your brain feels about to explode by the time you press send or hand something in, it may be time for you to be stricter with yourself (dare I use such a word to a perfectionist!) when it comes to time. At some point, you must have a cut-off, where you lay that task to rest - at least for the time being. You may need to be more disciplined about when you leave the office for the day, or how long you spend on an assignment. It will feel unnatural at first to stop something before you would usually feel compelled to, but both your schedule and your mental health will thank you!

Get used to making mistakes: Ah, mistakes. Realistically, you won't exactly be welcoming them, but once they've already turned up unannounced, you may as well see what they have to say! Embracing that you will inevitably make mistakes and becoming more willing to learn from them is one of the most important things you can learn. However, perfectionists hate making mistakes. But because they don't allow themselves to make them, and when they do they refuse to learn anything from them as they are too busy punishing themselves, they may miss out on vital opportunities to learn and grow.

Understand the real issue: When most people "confess" to being a perfectionist, they wear it as some sort of badge of honor. The problem is, perfectionism is nothing more than a label we place on ourselves to hide the fact that we are deeply afraid of failure. Afraid of what others will think. Even, afraid of success. The last one sounds peculiar, but think about this - what does a perfectionist do once they have "made it"? Once they eventually achieve that near-impossible goal that they were living and breathing for? Do you think they basque in the exhilaration of it all? Unlikely. They usually immediately look towards the next milestone. And then the next, and the next. For a perfectionist, nothing is ever enough. And so, they live their lives in some sort of furlough between hurdles they set out for themselves, but never allowing themselves to celebrate each one as it is achieved.

If you worry that this is you, the easiest way to overcome fear is to face it head on. Don't obsess over what could happen, or how things might not work out - if you feel compelled to try, then go for it! Failure often isn't as painful as the anticipation of it - and the blow is softened by the satisfaction that you tried, and have now learned something about how to improve next time.

The Bottom Line

As a society, we struggle to deal with the unusual and the unknown. We often choose to stick to a tried-and-tested formula, rather than take the risk and create a new one for ourselves. As a result, we favor those who stick to the rules rather than those bold enough to rewrite them - even if these are the people who end up being the most influential in the end. In this quest for familiarity, reassurance, and validation, we reject the slightest deviation from the paths we lay out for ourselves. Any unexpected result or setback, any mistake we make along the way, is interpreted as a disaster - rather than the natural bump in the road that it is.

Having unrealistic expectations about ourselves contributes to increased anxiety, depression, and general life dissatisfaction. This self-targeting perfectionism is usually the result of trying to live up to a self-inflicted unrealistic ideal, but it can also be motivated by the fear of failure or judgment from others.

Of course, setting high standards for ourselves inspires us to do the very best that we can to achieve our potential and to approach life with motivation and ambition. As such, a certain level of perfectionism can be healthy in this regard, but when it becomes unhealthy and disruptive, it can cause serious problems both to mental health and to – ironically – your performance.

Extreme perfectionists tend to be overthinkers as they approach their life with an "all or nothing" mentality. But the world isn't all black and white! Most things in life, and most things you will do during your life, are not a binary in this way. Things don't tend to be simply "good" or" bad," as everything is filled with nuance and complexity. As such, if we live our life scrutinizing every shade of grey and categorizing it as either black or white, not only is this an utter waste of time and mental energy, but we will drive ourselves mad in the process.

Managing perfectionism often requires changing the way you perceive life – both success and failure. Just because things don't go 100% as you planned them, or if things didn't go exactly as you wanted, doesn't mean that you should write it off as a failure. Rather, see what did go right and acknowledge what you learned from the experience. Learn to be able to walk away from something that you don't deem "perfect" and feel at ease, realizing that perfection isn't natural, and often not even desirable. We're all just winging things as we go along, after all! Excellence, on the other hand, encourages this drive and ambition, and yet leaves room for the mistakes you will make, the deviations in the road, and acknowledges the full scope that "success" can truly mean.

Chapter 6

Indecisiveness and how to fight it

One of the key occasions where we tend to overthink is when it comes to making decisions - however big or small. Many people who have a tendency to overthink make the mistake of trying to predict all possible scenarios and only end up getting stuck by ending up deliberating over it so much that they lose clarity.

When you're not confident about a decision you're making, it's tempting to just avoid it altogether. Perhaps you've become indecisive due to a specific trauma, insecurity, or distraction. Alternatively, maybe you've simply always lived in fear of making the "wrong" choice or doing the "wrong" thing. Regardless of the root cause of your indecisiveness, it likely leaves you feeling frustrated and even powerless. But what can you do to take ownership of your freedom to choose, and stop being so indecisive?

Overthinkers tend to struggle to make decisions because they don't have enough faith in their ability to think for themselves; they believe that other people are more capable than themselves when it comes to making the "right" choice. In this scenario, you may feel compelled to always consult others who you trust more than yourself, in order to feel more confident in their decisions. The problem here is that this gives other people control, when sometimes you simply have to make your own choices, free from the influences of others. This is for your own good - for your self-esteem just as much as for your sense of autonomy. If you continuously hand over responsibility for your own decisions to others, you forfeit your own control and authority. You must learn to trust yourself by cultivating adequate self-belief and self-confidence. No one else can replace your own authority in your life. Some things, you must learn to do for yourself.

One way to beat overthinking is to beat indecision. To take control of your choices rather than handing them over to others. This will give you a sense of increased confidence and clarity when it comes to taking action in your life.

Why do you struggle so much to make decisions?

The curse of indecisiveness

But why is it that some people seem to struggle to make even the smallest decisions - such as which shampoo to buy or what to make for dinner? Health and Wellness Expert, Caleb Backe, stated the following:

"Some people can't/don't make decisions because they are too busy over-analyzing everything. They analyze things to death, and are satisfied with that. They justify to themselves that they are not ignoring the problems. Quite the opposite — they are always thinking about them. But while thought is a wonderful thing, it is best coupled with an action. That jump from theoretical to practical is one which has a strong element of risk and danger in it. Some thrive on that feeling, but most of us are not ready to deal with it in many areas of our life."

If you are a member of this over-analyzing, overthinking, indecisive club, then fear not. You at least can never be accused of running away from your problems! However, as with most things, balance is key. Just as you shouldn't avoid thinking about important things in your life, you also shouldn't become consumed by every

single decision you have to make. It's estimated that the average adult makes about 35,000 remotely conscious decisions each day. Granted - some of these even overthinkers will make almost on instinct - such as whether to smile at a stranger, or whether you walk around or straight through a puddle in your path - but can you even imagine how much time and mental energy you could save by not agonizing over even just half of these decisions?

Decision Fatigue explained
How even the smallest decisions can be draining your mental energy

Research into the psychology of indecisiveness reveals a whole host of negative repercussions, with it limiting your success in everything; from your career to your personal relationships. Furthermore, there appear to be diverse causes of this struggle. As such, whatever causes indecisiveness in you may not be the same thing that provokes it in someone else. However, there are certain key sources to look for that that commonly impact one's ability to independently make decisions:

Living to Please

The core of your indecisiveness may lie in trying too hard to please other people. You might think that if you sit back and let others get their own way, then you'll get more approval, and external validation. As already discussed, depending too heavily on the opinions of others for your own sense of self-worth and direction is inherently harmful and takes away your own sense of self and autonomy. Essentially, if you get into the habit of letting everyone else go before you while you remain passive when it comes to making a decision, your self-belief and ability to make your own choices only further weakens with time.

Broken Self-Trust

Alternatively, after a procession of bad choices or simply negative outcomes that you blame on your own decisions, you may lose faith in your own judgment as a consequence. A lack of self-belief and self-trust can be debilitating, as you know longer allow yourself to have any sort of authority on decisions - big or small. It may be that you made one too many work mistakes for you to feel you can forgive yourself, or maybe whatever you wear leaves you feeling embarrassed.

Paralysis of Choice

And then there's the concept of choice-paralysis, coined by French philosophers in the 20th century. The idea is that we are faced with so many choices in the developed world today - more so now than ever before - that we can actually feel paralyzed as a result - unable to choose just one of the many options. Whether it's the endless brands of the same simple product at the supermarket, the endless career or studying opportunities that lie before you, or the unfathomable amount of potential people to seek a relationship with thanks to the internet connecting us to more people than ever before - it can be overwhelming to even think about choosing just one anything. Working out how to make up your mind can be that much harder when you're literally spoilt for choice.

The 40/70 Rule of Decision-Making

The ultimate trick to stop overthinking your decisions

An excellent approach to consider to beat your indecisiveness is Colin Powell's 40/70 rule. Once we have established whether we have gathered the information necessary to make an informed choice, we then - in theory - use our instincts to avoid thinking about it too much. Our ability to become successful marketers, leaders, managers, or entrepreneurs depends upon this crucial ability to make informed and yet not over-thought choices on a constant basis.

From designing a new product to making a bold business or strategic move, most career paths are rife with continuous decisions. On top of that, the outcomes can have huge effects down the line, only adding to the pressure of our choices. And just as some thrive on the sense of power provided by this, for others, it can send your head into a spin, as every step you take, you feel the need to look closely at the ground before gingerly placing your foot... Research has proven that the best leaders are those who have the ability to make important decisions, both thoughtfully and confidently. The point is: anybody can make "snap decisions" -and these aren't often advised - however, to do so both quickly and effectively is the hack we all need.

Enter: The 40/70 rule

Here's the thing: every single choice that you make is composed of a range of elements - such as your own self-confidence, your understanding of the issue at hand, your experience in the subject, and your determination to be proactive and take action. The threshold for all of these components to come together and assist in the arrival at a definitive decision is where things can get a little more complicated...

The previous US Secretary of State, Colin Powell, came up with something called the 40/70 rule. The idea behind it is that when you have between 40 and 70% of the details needed to make a decision, this is when you are best equipped to make a choice. No more, no less.

Try to make a decision with less than 40% of the information, and you're stabbing in the dark. But wait until you have more than 70% of the info, and you find that you actually waited for too long, and may now end up being overwhelmed which leads to indecisiveness.

The 40/70 rule comes in two parts in its approach to decision-making. Powell specifies that you do require a sufficient level of information in order to make an informed choice on the matter - but not so much that you run the risk-taking too long or beating around the bush, hesitating before you take the necessary action.

Part I: Determine Your Information Percentage

To get a better understanding of where exactly you fall into this elusive 40-70 range, Powell presents the following formula:

P = 40 to 70

Here, P equates to the likelihood of success, and the numbers indicate the portion of information that you have. While a definitive percentage can be hard to come up with, you need to approximate where you believe you fall within this window, based on exactly what details you have.

Part II: Trust Your Instincts

After you've reached that sweet spot between 40 and 70 percent, it's then up to your instincts to make the final decision. This part is what distinguishes the leaders from the crowd, because it's not exclusively about the facts -

but also involves your intrinsic impulse - and of course, your trust in it.

The Consequences of your Actions

Since there are consequences for every action, there are also long-reaching after-effects for inaction. This notion is what determines the minimum amount of information to make a choice, according to the 40-70 rule.

Making a decision when you have less than 40% of the information needed can result in a failure to acknowledge particular elements of the issue can lead you to make decisions that don't fully address the circumstances. On top of that, ill-informed choices can inflict unfavorable implications for either yourself, your project, or other people involved in this choice. And finally, you risk making an objectively incorrect decision that could have been avoided had you gotten more details before making it.

On the other hand, making a decision when you have more than 70% of the details needed can result in you overthinking every minute aspect of the issue, causing you to become lost in the details, and blind to the bigger picture. You may also experience this aforementioned phenomenon of choice paralysis, now that you are so immersed in all the different options and what they could mean, there is no one particular option that stands out to you. And so you continue to overthink, to deliberate, and things only decrease in clarity. You may never even manage to make a decision in the end as it all becomes too much! Or, you get so frustrated that you end up choosing one opinion on a whim, just so that the turmoil will end - and this only results in the same negative consequences of making an uninformed choice, as listed above.

So next time you're confronted with a predicament that requires a definitive answer, try approaching it with the 40/70 rule in mind, making sure that you're setting yourself up for the best possible outcomes. Of course, you're not always going to make the ideal call - as i hope you will remember from the last chapter, such perfection is not even possible! However, by using this formula combined with your gut instinct, you're most likely to maintain a constant, robust, and yet efficient decision-making process.

How to beat indecision

How to stop every decision being a huge affair.

What are some more concrete steps you can take from today to help your frazzled, decision-fatigued mind, and clear up a little more space for the important stuff? Here are some interesting tactics you could consider:

Don't sweat the small stuff

Do you know what Barack Obama and Mark Zuckerberg have in common (besides being American, and high achievers that is)? They both have been known to wear pretty much the exact same thing every single day: Obama sports a dark blue suit, and Zuckerberg a grey tee-shirt. And they do this for the same intriguing reason: to spare their overworked minds of one less little decision each day.

As discussed previously, we only have a limited amount of mental energy in a given day – and this, of course, still applies if you're the former leader of the free world or the founder of one of the world's most well-known companies!

You have probably experienced yourself when you simply can't form an opinion anymore. Often, it's the small stuff that won't inflict drastic consequences either way – what to have for breakfast, what film to watch, or indeed – what clothes to put on each day. We all have so much else going on in our overworked brains that we can end up hitting a wall when presented with a less important decision that we have no strong opinion about either way. It's as though our minds have given up – they may jump into gear if suddenly presented with an emergency or pressing matter – but sometimes it's the trivial stuff that we struggle with the most. Psychologists call this phenomenon "decision fatigue."

Roy F. Baumeister, a psychologist specialized in decision fatigue, told the New York Times:

'Making decisions uses the very same willpower that you use to say no to doughnuts, drugs, or illicit sex. It's the same willpower that you use to be polite or to wait your turn or to drag yourself out of bed or to hold off going to the bathroom. Your ability to make the right investment or hiring decision may be reduced simply because you expended some of your willpower earlier when you held your tongue in response to someone's offensive remark or when you exerted yourself to get to the meeting on time.'

And as Obama notoriously confessed to Vanity Fair back in 2012 while he was still in office, surviving as a key political figure without your brain exploding requires that you throw out the more mundane decisions such as deciding what to wear, or what to have for breakfast - which others may cloud their minds with - every single morning. He stated:

'You'll see I wear only grey or blue suits. I'm trying to pare down decisions. I don't want to make decisions about what I'm eating or wearing. Because I have too many other decisions to make.'

Facebook founder, Mark Zuckerberg had a similar take, stating: 'I really want to clear my life to make it so that I have to make it so that I have to make as few decisions as possible about anything except how to best serve this community.'

Okay, I'm not suggesting we all go around wearing the same thing every single day so that everywhere looks like a dystopian "Black Mirror" episode and self-expression and creativity become a crime. This technique works more for some than for others. And if you get a great deal of joy and self-expression out of what you wear, then you do you! But I encourage you to distinguish important decisions from more minor ones. Prioritize where you spend your mental energy. This is done with the aim of not occupying our whole mind for less important choices - for example, giving ourselves short time for small decisions, or limiting the options we have - in order to provide more time to the most critical decisions that require more rigorous reflection. I must reiterate the benefit of putting a deadline on our decisions to avoid constant overthinking. Start by setting short time-limits for small decisions, as well as some sort of deadline, even for bigger decisions.

Tune Into Your Emotions

As an overthinking and indecisive person, one of the first things you must try to do is to stop over-analyzing. Easier said than done, I know. This tendency comes from the fact you don't trust your instincts, which, as I mentioned earlier, is a vital part of becoming empowered. Consequently, if you work on more deeply tuning into your emotions, you'll develop your intrinsic finely honed intuitions (yes, we all have them, but many of us forget!) that help you confidently make choices without over-analyzing.

Whether you want to learn how to stop being indecisive in your relationships with others, or are thinking more about your career or wider life choices, being more emotionally aware can help in all of these areas. You must ask whether your hesitation is due to a deep fear of not being prepared or capable enough, or an anxiety of what could happen if you make the wrong choice - causing you to shake under the weight of all the potential outcomes - good and bad.

If it's fear of incapacity, simply proceed with one manageable step at a time. Learn from each one and keep moving forward. Your confidence and self-belief will solidify as you go on, making it easier and easier to trust yourself and take action each time. If it's anxiety of the unknown, then jump right in - put yourself in a position where you don't have the luxury of time to overthink. It seems harsh, but it may be the only way to kickstart yourself into action and break the habit of senseless rumination. So make a commitment you can't back down from. Accept your anxiety as something that will come and go, and power through anyway.

Of course, this may sound good in theory, but how do you reliably put it into practice? Try proving the worth of your intuitions by making a list of five times in life when your gut instinct was right. Maybe it was your first impressions of an individual who has since made an impact in your life. Or maybe it was a work decision or an important lifestyle change that ended up working out for the best in the long-run. Whatever it is, cultivate a broader self-awareness by keeping a daily journal and reflecting on your emotions, your gut feelings, and your predictions. Even just a few minutes spent doing this each day can help you vastly by tapping into those reflective and intuitive capacities that have long been dormant or ignored.

Learn To Trust Yourself

Overcoming indecisiveness is also about finding your unique strengths and figuring out how you can apply them to help your decision-making process.

If you're like most of my clients who struggle with indecision, you might find it difficult to pinpoint your strengths. After all, this in itself requires a certain level of confidence and self-awareness that indecisive individuals often lack in the first place. But trust me - even if it isn't clear, I am certain that you have many useful and applicable personal strengths. And it's about time you harnessed their potential!

Try to list at least five of your main strengths. Think of the strengths others have acknowledged in you. Are you well-organized, a very personable individual, or maybe you have a particular way with numbers or with words? Perhaps you're known for your unique sense of humor or your unfailing optimism in times of difficulty. Take your time to really think it through - reflecting on your past achievements, experiences, and interactions with others.

Next, think of at least one way that each of these specific strengths could be used to facilitate your decision-making. For example, optimism can be used to increase your confidence of making a choice by reminding you that you can survive any outcome of the decision, anyway. Meanwhile, your interpersonal skills may mean that you can talk your way out of any situation, or always rely on communicating with others to receive support if things don't go to plan.

Visualize All Possible Outcomes

When figuring out how to make difficult life decisions, although too much can be risky for overthinkers, visualization takes you closer to the reality of the different options. This can then make the right choice for you become much clearer and offer some much-needed reassurance that a decision isn't as foreboding as you feared. If you already have some experience with visualization - for example, via mindfulness meditation, as I will get into more deeply later in this book - you'll find that this technique comes pretty naturally.

That being said, even if you're totally new to visualization and aren't really sure what I mean by it, you can pick it up quickly. Simply close your eyes and breathe deeply until you feel relaxed. Allow yourself to detach slightly from your reality - all preconceived biases and ideas. All worries about what others may decide, or what you feel you should decide. Just focus on you and your own gut feeling. Then, use your imagination to hypothetically embed yourself in all the possible choices before you. Notice how you feel in each scenario. Which one feels the most natural, or that puts you most at ease? Trust your instinct to guide you to the right one.

If this kind of creative visualization really doesn't work for you or just sounds a bit abstract, there are other approaches you may prefer. For instance, try drawing up a mind map as another way of visualizing your options, but in a more linear and logical way for those who are more that way inclined. But be careful that this strategy doesn't veer off into over-analysis...

Take Your Own Sweet Time

While I have already laid our reasons why you should sometimes set time limits when making decisions, there are some cases where taking your time is preferable. For instance, new psychological research reveals that if you take a short break from thinking about a choice, you often end up making a better thought-out decision. This links to what I pointed out earlier about changing up your environment in order to feed creativity and mental clarity. The same applies here.

The issue is that we can sometimes become entrapped by paranoia about making a decision under time pressure, and this can create additional anxiety. The anxiety, and the brain fog and panic implicated, then makes it almost impossible to single out one choice. When you feel that this might be happening to you, put the decision aside for a while. Allow your mind to wander onto other things as you focus on something else for a while, take a short break or a quick walk. See how much more clear-minded and calm you feel once you return to thinking about the decision.

Take Action

When overcoming a history or simply a bout of indecisiveness, it's important to remember that you can learn from both your successes, and from your mistakes. In other words - even if you mess up and make the "wrong" choice from time to time, remember that you're human and not a machine. Buckle up and try it again. You will develop both your experience and your confidence with time, regardless of the mistakes you make along the way.

Learning what works for you, personally, is a process of trial and error in itself, that relies on your own willingness to put yourself out there and experiment. It's only when you attempt different techniques, like the ones discussed above, that you'll actually be able to determine what will push you towards better and more effective decision-making.

Additionally, try to make a habit of willingly stepping outside of your comfort zone. Step up and take action in every area of your life, rather than exclusively the areas you feel particularly comfortable with. And do this while bearing in mind that you can make something good away from every possible result - whether or not things go as you planned, as long as you open yourself up to new opportunities for learning and growing. When you see things this way, it's a win-win! You either succeed, or you learn how to better succeed next time. Because, even when things don't turn out as you'd expected or would have liked, this is what provides the most fertile soil for healthy growth. In truth, it is often those lessons we learn from our most gut-wrenching mistakes that lead us to something better in the future. So slowly allow yourself to become more at ease and accustomed to putting yourself out there - stepping up to new challenges, trying new things, and pushing your self-imposed limits. If you want something in your life to change, the first change starts with your own actions, after all. Feeding your own resilience, adaptability, and versatility in this way is one of the most effective ways to prove to yourself that you have the power to own your decisions and handle whatever comes your way as a result of them.

The Bottom Line

I should probably finish by pointing out that indecision isn't always bad. Sometimes, hesitation before making a choice gives you valuable time to think about the whole situation. If you can't seem to arrive at an answer quickly, it may just be a sign that what's at stake really matters to you, and you rightfully don't want to mess up. This need for extended thought and reflection is, of course, necessary from time to time. The most important thing is to not let indecision keep you stuck forever. Deliberate when you need to, but you have to make a choice eventually. And although some decisions may take more time and analysis than others, don't allow yourself to become completely paralyzed every time you are presented with a fork in your path.

Make no mistake: Indecision becomes a disruptive thing when it lasts for too long. How long is too long, you may ask? Well, that depends on the specific context and circumstances. Will you miss an important opportunity by waiting? Could you lose something potentially very valuable just because of your hesitation? Is the decision getting harder or easier to make, the more time and energy you spend dwelling on it?

On top of that, indecision can sometimes become a decision by default. For instance, if you decide not to decide, you essentially forfeit your power of choice. Someone else might get chosen for that opportunity you spent so long mulling over, or another buyer might snap up that property you couldn't make your mind up about, but may have actually been your dream home.

Only you hold the keys to changing your mindset; Perhaps you have already labeled yourself an "indecisive person," but don't let this define you. You may have moments of indecisiveness or hesitance, but that's a habit you can overcome, not a personality trait! You can learn to make decisions, just like you learned to read or ride a bike. It's just a skill like any other.

If you don't start to take initiative within your own life, you'll only end up becoming a prisoner of your own indecisiveness. You'll limit your opportunities, not allowing yourself to be open to changes that could enhance your life and pave the way towards you achieving your goals and aspirations. To finish with a quote by Denis Waitley:

'Life is inherently risky. There is only one big risk you should avoid at all costs, and that is the risk of doing nothing.'

Chapter 7

Procrastination cure

We all procrastinate from time to time - "I'll do it later" or "I can't start until I do x, y, and z," - but most of us don't really consider the reasons why we do this, or consider that it can actually be linked to anxiety and overthinking - rather than just laziness.

Overthinking, unfortunately, has a close link with low productivity. We often postpone tasks to be carried out until we really cannot put it off anymore, although knowing that these are important and should be carried out immediately. This behavior is due primarily to factors such as fear of failure, perfectionism, and incorrect organization of the task and thoughts - but it actually only increases your anxiety and fear of failure, as you end up having to rush something at the last minute and when under duress, rather than taking your time so that you can produce your best word.

Am I just a lazy bastard?

The difference between laziness and executive

I will get into some of the common reasons beyond procrastination later on, but first of us, we need to rule out one thing. Are you just being lazy? Is there a deeper reason for your putting off of this task, or is this all it boils down to. Essentially, are you experiencing an executive function (a non-deliberate failure to do things on time), or an executive dysfunction (a deliberate "putting things off until later" situation)?

Let me explain a little better.

Executive function is the process of identifying, planning, executing, and following through with tasks. And so, if you have a dysfunction regarding any of these components - that would imply an executive dysfunction. This implies that rather than being a procrastinator, there is actually another underlying cause.

For instance, it could be that you have an issue with figuring out what needs to be done or where to even begin. You may have difficulty managing your time, and so can't map out a time when exactly you can do something. Lastly, you may simply be disorganized - perhaps because your brain is so cluttered with your overthinking habit - that you struggle to even remember the tasks you need to do. You end up frazzled and having to catch up, or feel overwhelmed and simply feel unable to face the task once you remember that it exists.

All of this, as well as countless other scenarios, are examples of executive dysfunction. There is some part of your productivity chain that is lacking, and this is why your work isn't getting done as it should be.

Procrastination, on the other hand, is a deliberate choice. This is when you have an executive function but are not getting your tasks done because you are putting them off. You don't want to do your assignment, go to the gym, or read that report, so you don't. Of course, even this isn't simple. You may truly want to do these things deep down for the long-term benefits you would reap - you know it's the right thing to do - but something is stopping you. At the end of the day, it is still a conscious choice not to do it - but there could be an unconscious reason behind this choice.

The Roots of Procrastination

Why do you really put off the work you need to do?

As mentioned, procrastination is a conscious decision to put something off until later, to prioritize your short-term comfort for your long-term gain. Now, this could be just because you really don't want to do the task at hand - or, for no other reason than that, it's hard and you can't be bothered. However, what many people don't realize is that there is often an underlying root to your procrastination in any one instance - even if you are not conscious of it at the time. The most likely sources of your procrastination are fear, disorganization, and perfectionism, which can then be further divided into several principal causes.

They go as follows:

Procrastination due to your memory being overwhelmed

For example, you get overwhelmed by all the tasks firing your way at work. There seem to be so many things that you need to do, that you can hardly manage to focus on just one. This links to what I discussed in an earlier chapter about sticking to one task until it's complete, and not falling for the myth of multitasking. But sometimes, when you feel like you're completely swimming in requests and demands, this is quite the exercise for your mental concentration and certainly easier said than done...

If you're anything like my clients, even noting things down on a calendar or diary can feel overwhelming, as you end up with a messy visualization of all the chaos in your mind. The solution to this is to find a way to schedule your time, separate chunks of your time to concentrate wholly on specific tasks, so your mind doesn't become overcrowded, and to find a way to remind yourself only once it becomes necessary of the next oncoming task. Electronic calendar alerts or project management tools are great for this, as it will only show specific alerts when you actually need to see them.

Procrastination due to fear of the unknown

Fear of uncertainty or anything unfamiliar is another common cause of anxiety problems which can also feed into your procrastination habit. Do you have a general tendency to feel stuck whenever you feel uncertain about doing something? Or perhaps you obsess over where to start to such a point that you become fearful to even approach the task?

Similarly, do you tend to overthink every possible scenario before you take that first step? If this is the case, you run the risk of getting caught up in details rather than grasping the big picture.

Procrastination due to unrealistic standards and expectations

As touched upon earlier, black-and-white, all-or-nothing thinking is a surefire way to leave you battling anxiety and overthinking. But how can this lead you to procrastinate? Could you save yourself some unnecessary stress by doing a task you've been avoiding, yet in a way more in line with where you feel comfortable and like you can perform your best? For instance, could you break it into small chunks rather than attempting the whole thing at once?

Or maybe there's a way you can put your own spin on the task, to make it somehow more "your own" - which can not only allow you to tap into your flow state but will likely result in a much more passion-fed and therefore high-quality result. Obviously, there's not always much room for adaptation, depending on the task. But there often is more flexibility than you may have been thinking - and a way to make the task seem less daunting.

Sometimes it's not an all-or-nothing scenario - you can complete a task yet in a more creative, or at least in a more comfortable way. To give this a go in a more relatable sense, try to identify just one task that you're dreading that you'd be less likely to avoid if you reduced your or changed your standards - as well as what kinds of standards you can realistically afford to adapt.

Procrastination due to negative assumptions

It's often the case that when someone drags their heels on a task, it's quite simply because they're predicting a negative outcome. If you have already convinced yourself that something won't work, or will end in failure, then it makes you less enthusiastic about attempting it. Your subconscious is simply trying to spare you the trouble! But the catch is that we often get it wrong - we can't always predict what an outcome will be. I'm sure you can recall times where you were sure something would fail, only to be pleasantly surprised. Well, imagine if you never even tried? You would still be convincing yourself that it wasn' with attempting.

The truth is, half the battle is noticing that you're making a negative prediction - as it can often be unconscious Recognise first of all, as I discuss at length (especially in my last book on self-confidence!) that failure is not your enemy anyway. It can be your best teacher. But also realize that a negative outcome is only one of the possible outcomes. Try the three questions technique, where you identify three potential outcomes: the worst, the best, and finally - the most realistic. By imagining the worst and best-case scenarios first, you will be better able to determine the most likely outcome - that almost always comes somewhere in the middle, and isn't as bad as you'd feared.

Procrastination due to lack of drive

This is another topic I discussed at length in my last book on self-confidence. One key component of your self-belief - that often goes overlooked, even within positive psychology "self-development" circles, is self-efficacy. In case you aren't;t familiar with this term, self-efficacy refers to your drive. You may be a confident person who still is lacking in this department. That's because self-efficacy is focused on your actions rather than your thoughts or intentions. For instance, someone who talks themselves up gloats about the businesses they will start, the places they will travel to, or the goals they have maybe a self-confident person with some big aspirations. However, it is self-efficacy that actually makes you get up and do those things. To make your dreams a reality outside of your own head...

And so, if you feel this may be what you are lacking, then know that you are already halfway there! If you're the type to make big plans but not always follow them through, then first recognize that the fact that you have big plans and know what you want to do is already a great step. Next, focus on what exactly is preventing you from actually taking the leap to get the ball rolling on these big plans... The next section may help you with this.

The Types of Procrastination

So you now know whether you have a procrastination rather than simply an executive dysfunction problem. And if the former, you may have even determined the main source of your procrastination. But this isn't the full story. How does your procrastination manifest? That's what we will delve into next:

Anxious-Perfectionist Procrastinator

As an overthinker, it's pretty likely that your procrastination is laced with anxiety. This could either stem from your perfectionism, as already discussed, making you put off tasks until you have perfect conditions, perfect background knowledge, or won't submit something until it meets your unrealistically perfect expectations. Although many may believe that these perfectionist types are more productive than most, it can actually hinder your productivity, as you may delay processes and not actually complete things on time as they never seem to be good enough for you.

Stanford University Philosopher, John Perry, proposes that procrastinating can actually be a good thing for perfectionists…

'As long as they have a lot of time to do a task, they fantasize about doing a perfect job. Leaving it till the last minute is a way of giving oneself permission to do a merely adequate job. 99% of the time, a merely adequate job is all that is needed.'

Try looking back at the last five tasks you completed. Were they all perfect, honestly? Were they good enough, though? The chances are, if you have overthinking and perfectionist tendencies, that you're already working to a high standard even when you don't think you are - so stop giving yourself such a hard time!

Identifying those times where you didn't do such a perfect job, but the consequences were just the same as though you had, will help you to overcome your perfectionist routine and stop procrastinating. Sometimes good is good enough!

Exhausted Procrastinator

Another common type of procrastination is simply down to your own well-being. This often goes hand-in-hand with anxiety-fuelled procrastination. It basically means you are so overworked or overburdened, that you are not physically or mentally your best. You may be sleep-deprived, malnourished, dehydrated, or simply starved of downtime. Whatever it is, how can you expect to perform your best when your most basic needs are not met? If you procrastinate, you may feel guilty about downtime as you are plagued with thoughts of all the things you really ought to be doing. But without adequate rest, we can't achieve anything. We are not machines!

And so, to overcome this type of procrastination, you may need to actually incorporate downtime into your busy schedule. It could be "social media time," "call-a-friend time," "read a chapter time," or even "Netflix time"! Whatever you need to unwind and feel ready for the next onslaught of work. It isn't anything to feel guilty about. And once it is officially incorporated into your schedule, you won't feel so deprived during your actual working time. Like a kid, don't deprive them of fun, and they will likely behave a lot better!

Fun-Seeking Procrastinator

On the reverse side, and yet still on a related note, the fun-seeking procrastinator would rather be doing literally anything except that one dreaded task that they're supposed to be working on. And the more they think about what they should be doing, the more impossible it becomes to drag themselves away from their preferred pastime... Now, if there's simply no way that you're ever going to start on that one so-dreaded task, at the very least, have a go at indulging in some more structured procrastination. This may not be what you expected - but if you're going to procrastinate anyway, why not make it on your own terms? Allow yourself to procrastinate a little and on your terms (see above), but once your fun-time is over and you still can't focus, then start another item on your to-do list.

Often, by avoiding this particular task - even if you are only replacing it with another -, you get that same sense of satisfaction and may even come back to it feeling more able, having managed to tick off something else on your list. Procrastination and productivity in one, I hear you say? Double win.

Directionless Procrastinator

Most people find it to be an uphill struggle to start a project when the deadline seems like it is a long way off. There's an absence of a sense of urgency or immediate obligation that many of us require to jump into action. Indeed, sometimes a little pressure is actually good for us as it keeps us moving forward without too much dilly-dallying. And then there are those tasks you know need to get done, but that don't have a deadline at all - which can be especially hard to get down to.

To overcome this "lost" feeling when there is a loose or non-existent lime limit, try setting your own deadlines and noting them down - even saying them aloud either to someone else (who will listen!) or simply to yourself. This active commitment and the associated sense of obligation that comes along with it may actually be all it takes to keep you on track and motivate you to keep your head in the game until you meet those deadlines you set for yourself.

Sabotaging your Self-sabotaging behaviours

Are you self-sabotaging without realising it?

Have you ever found that things are going well for you - either in your career, your relationship, or perhaps just your overall contentment - only for you to do something inexplicable that damages the success you're reaping and forces you back a few steps? You stop putting the effort in at work, or blow up with your partner or loved one for no good reason? Or, maybe you mentally berate yourself when you're in the midst of an important challenge. This could make you feel increasingly discouraged and frustrated, and angry at yourself, which prevents you from reaching your potential, achieving the desired mental state of "flow," and doing whatever it is that you need to do for your own self-development and success. All of these behaviors indicate that you may be unknowingly self-sabotaging.

Worrying, I know - aren't we supposed to be on our own side? The subconscious mind is cruel like that.

Sabotage is defined as 'the act of destroying or undermining something.' The term self-sabotage, then, is used when this destructive behavior is directed at yourself. Self-sabotage eats away at your self-confidence and self-esteem. And insidiously, with every failed attempt to complete a task or achieve something as you set out to, you unconsciously feel you have "proven" to yourself that you can't or shouldn't continue... You may not even be aware that you're doing this to yourself. However, when negative habits consistently throw your efforts off course - either at work or regarding your health and relationships - they can be considered a form of psychological self-harm.

Self-sabotage can manifest in many different behaviors, unique to each person. For instance, you might repeatedly "forget" your deadlines, or be consistently late to work. You may fail to prepare for a presentation or test adequately. In your personal life, you may keep making unhealthy choices you know you shouldn't, or push people away once they show affection for you.

Maybe you start projects but never finish them. You convince yourself, presented with an exciting opportunity, that you don't want to go for it, or that it's a stupid idea.

Self-sabotage is driven by self-destructive inner monologues. Basically, you tell yourself that you don't want something (when you do) or that you can't do something (when you can!). You find yourself thinking things like, "that's a stupid idea anyway," "is it really worth the effort?" or "why try?"

We've likely all acted out like this at some point. As I hope you will remember from the last chapter - perfection is a myth! However, some of us are more prone to self-sabotage than others, and the fact that it can be difficult to admit - even to ourselves - that we're doing it makes it even harder to identify and thus manage.

From my own experience, one of the main factors leading my clients' self-sabotage is a lack of self-esteem. Self-esteem and reasons why it may be low is a whole other issue (which you can find out more about in my last book on self-confidence if you haven't already!), but all you need to know in this context is that the effects of low self-esteem are largely predictable: feelings of worthlessness, the misled belief that you don't deserve happiness or success due to ruminating on past mistakes or negative feedback, and even a dangerous level of self-loathing. It's common among those with low self-esteem to worry that if they fail at something, their loved ones will think less of them - or that if they're successful, it won't last. And so, they act out to take control of what they deem the inevitable. To the subconscious mind, sabotaging your own happiness is better than someone else doing so...

In this way, self-sabotage is another kind of vicious cycle, as it reinforces this misplaced sense of worthlessness and inadequacy, and provides justification for negative thoughts that feed back into the behavior. It provides an escape route when things seem to be turning south - even if only in your mind. And if you are worried that something won't end well, it's a way of saying "look, I didn't want this anyway" to seemingly spare yourself the humiliation of seeming to care.

So, how to fix this? As you become more aware of the negative feelings, behaviors, and thought-processes that trigger your self-sabotage habit, you can begin to challenge them with more positive and more rational affirmations. Then, try to link this new positive inner monologue to what you can accomplish and what you truly want to achieve - your insecurities and fears set to one side. This can help to turn your irrational assumptions around and gain some much-needed perspective.

Tips or advice to facilitate your productivity are all well and good, but at the end of the day, action is what actually gets things done.

Anti-procrastination techniques revealed

How to beat the all-or-nothing mentality.

For many, their procrastination stems from not caring enough. If you're not passionate about the work or feel that there is a greater purpose behind it that you find motivating, then it can be genuinely really difficult to apply yourself in spite of your daily distractions. As such, if procrastination is a persistent issue for you, consider if the underlying purpose - or lack thereof - of your work could be the reason.

Maybe, you're not lazy at all, or even particularly anxious. Rather, you are just looking for passion - and that's pretty commendable if you ask me! Just make sure you use this to your advantage and allow it to drive you to find a project or path that you can feel excited about.

That being said, sometimes you may actually have something to do that you simply must power through. We can't be excited all the time. That would make even excitement lose its excitement, I guess...

However, if your overall well-being and sense of purpose is in check, then those times where you have less enthralling, niggling tasks to complete won't seem so burdensome. You will be able to get your head down, get the work done, and come out of it feeling accomplished and ready to take on the tasks you find more enjoyable.

Laziness is different from procrastination - as it's possible to have one without the other. However, the same solutions for solving laziness can also be applied to procrastination in many cases. Here are five key tips for overcoming laziness-related procrastination:

Use the Two-minute Rule

Whenever you've got a task that you're thinking of putting off for later, ask yourself the following simple question: How long will this take? If the answer is two minutes or less, then do it straight away! This principle can also be applied to taller tasks because most tasks take less than two minutes to be set in motion - and then the rest will seem more achievable as you already made the first step.

Start Immediately - Think Later

Often, we commit self-sabotage in the subtle way of doing other things before work. Of course,

starting is often the most dreaded part - especially if you're dealing with chronic laziness or procrastination. So I say just start.

You can actually trick your mind to starting work. Try telling yourself that you'll only spend the first five minutes or so working before doing that other thing that's luring you away - like checking your social media or making coffee. The chances are that once you're already stuck in and on a roll, you'll realize that those things can wait.

Ignore Your Distractions

In most situations, you can't avoid distractions, but you can ignore them if you really want to. For instance, if your co-workers discuss what happened at the bar last night, your friend is texting you about their love life, simply block out these distractions - you can engage later once your important work is done!

You can also block out certain notifications or put your phone on flight-mode if this is an easier way for you to remain focused. Just realize that most distractions can actually be muted if you truly want to - but that's another matter altogether!

The Bottom Line: Time To Be On Your Own Side!

This may not be something you want to hear, but the main cure to procrastination and laziness is taking action. So while the above-mentioned tips will work for some people, it may not work for others.

If you've tried a lot of things mentioned above - from setting calendar alerts, to taking scheduled breaks, to muting your social media, and are still having difficulties, then perhaps you just need to make an honest decision to start taking action on the things that matter to you.

However, once you are aware of the causes, the types, and the different possible manifestations of procrastination, as well as its link to self-sabotage, you are on the right track towards getting a handle on your own actions and productivity. Allowing yourself to take breaks or to reduce your expectations when necessary, but still being able to push yourself and learn to prioritize your time and mental energy to make your goals a reality, rather than floating dreams in your head! This way, you can fight your own corner, and be your own greatest coach and motivator - keeping any self-sabotaging behaviors at bay.

Stop! Stop! Stop!

Here I am again to interrupt your reading!

Just checking – if you haven't already!- if you could leave a short review on Amazon, letting me know what you like about this book!

I will really appreciate it! It would be an invaluable gift for a small writer like me.

I genuinely thank you!

Scan me for leaving a review!

Chapter 8

Mindfulness meditation

A great and effective way to relieve excessive overthinking is to do meditation and mindfulness exercises. This allows you to release any nervous tension accumulated during working hours or moments of high mental or emotional effort or difficulty. Furthermore, during this physical and mental activity, we learn not to think, as we usually constantly do, but to instead seek this sought-after mental and emotional state of flow - neither over nor under-stimulated - that we have gone over previously.

If you're a natural overthinker, then there's always something whirring around your brain, spurring your fight-or-flight response in the process and making you feel perpetually on edge, constantly ready to jump into action - which isn't good for your peace - or your blood pressure! Mindfulness and meditation could be the final missing jigsaw piece you're subconsciously searching for to reconnect with yourself and free yourself from this heavy mental burden.

Fix your body, fix your mind

The power of breathing and rest for mental clarity.

Meditation has blown up in the Western hemisphere during the past few years - from being almost solely associated with monks or hippies, to being a word that pops up daily as an inclusive practice that everyone is doing - or at the very least, thinking they ought to be doing!

But wait - don't write off meditation as dippy-hippy or reserved for California girls who go on Bali retreats. Meditation is beneficial for everyone and is actually much more straightforward and accessible once you see past all the "yogi" stereotypes of how you think someone who meditates should look or behave. There are actually many types of meditation and mindfulness exercises, as well as many medically proven neurological benefits (but more on that later…).

But what does true, neurologically nourishing, and non-performative meditation look like really? And how could it help you stop overthinking? Ray Dalio, American billionaire hedge fund manager, says the following regarding the impact of regular meditation on his life and success:

'When I look back at my life, I am happy to have had what most people would consider a successful life, not only regarding business but also in my relationships and in lots of ways. More than anything else, I attribute it to meditation—partially because of the creativity, partly because of the centeredness. TM has given me an ability to put things in perspective, which has helped a lot. I think meditation has been the single biggest influence on my life.'

In fact, many household names and leading CEOs attribute meditation and mindfulness to much of their success and ability to thrive - Oprah, Madonna, Arianna Huffington, and CEOs of LinkedIn (Jeff Weiner) and Ford Motors (Willian Clay) to name just a select few. Still need more convincing? How could meditation be incorporated into your own routine?

The main aim of meditation is to clear the mind and separate oneself from worldly or bodily distractions - from the mundane musings of what you're having for dinner or when your work is due, to the deeper stuff around your life's purpose or mistakes - meditation allows your mind a much-needed break that it seldom can't even get during sleep. This is traditionally supposed to enable you to reach a heightened level of awareness and inner peace. But now that the Buddhism-derived practice has become more mainstream even in western society, for many, it has become less of a spiritual practice, and more of a way to seek inner calm and a rest from the usual excessive thoughts. To reconnect with oneself and to attune oneself with the senses.

Overall, the ambiguity over the definition of meditation - with the focus more on the goal rather than the method - we are graciously left with a little wiggle room to tailor it to our own needs and preferences, making it work for us as we see fit. Of course, for some, this could well be preferable in the classic form of sitting in the lotus position with the palms facing upwards as they rest on the knees. However, for many, more creative exploration is required in order to truly sink into the intended restorative meditative state.

Perhaps the greatest appeal of meditation is that it is accessible to all, and requires no formal training or teacher. It's free, requires no fancy equipment or specific location - and yet, it is said to alleviate many of mental and emotional struggles – from anxiety and depression, to excessive overthinking. In fact, in various Asian civilizations, people have been meditating for thousands of years. Surely, there must be something to it, then!

Furthermore, the curious simplicity of meditation can be unnerving in a society riddled with products and hacks and noise. What do you mean you just sit there and do nothing? What do you watch? What do you listen to? What do I need to buy? Nothing. Yes, this can be enlightening in itself this day and age.

But I argue that as life gets busier, then meditation only becomes more profound. The more we do, the more special it is to do nothing.

So don't overthink meditation, at least! Don't waste time looking for elaborate techniques or methods. Just remember that "simple" doesn't necessarily mean "easy"... in fact, modern life has perhaps made "simple" the hardest thing of all for us to grasp. As such, meditation is both the ultimate challenge and the ultimate relief. As put by executive coach and pro-meditator Ravi Raman, 'its simplicity is a disguise.'

And so, meditation can be used as a way to reconnect with yourself and become more attuned to your bodily sensations and senses. It can be a great way to encourage your mind to temporarily slow down to stop its constant thinking for a brief moment that can, with repeated practice, improve your overthinking habit even when you're not engaging in the practice. It is essentially a way to close all the open tabs of your mind, as you would your computer (most of us have far too many in both contexts!). To reboot it. Don't lose sight of the fact that your mind is under constant strain, and overthinking is only further burdening it, making it more likely to crash or over-heat.

Meditation and mindfulness

How can meditation work for you?

And here's that word again: mindfulness.

It may sound contradictory to suggest incorporating something called "mindfulness" in order to make your mind less...well...full. However, mindfulness is all about allowing thoughts to come and go - acknowledging and being aware of every thought and emotion, yet not letting any of them stick around and sour into rumination. It's about, as touched upon previously, living in the moment. Feeling the oxygen flood your body with every breath, the breeze on your face, the warmth of your toes in your socks, and the faint chirping of birds in the distance. It's about sharpening your senses and yet not letting any of them overwhelm you.

The thing is, the modern way of life is full of contradictions. Just as we overstimulate our senses with screens and headphones and overthinking, we somehow also manage to become somewhat senorily numb when it comes to more organic stimulation - such as the triggers mentioned above. As such, our minds become cluttered with he-said-that's, and notifications, and emails, and advertisements - and yet leave no room for the more wholesome stimuli of nature, meaningful face-to-face conversations, and smiles from strangers. Is it any wonder our brains are frazzled with stimulation, and yet we still keep craving more?

Not only is mindfulness about learning to live in the present and stop constant mental "time travel," but it is an entire way of living and of being. Whether you adopt daily meditation, yoga, or tai chi ritual - or prefer a quiet walk on your lunch break - your overburdened brain is desperate for this moment to pause and detach from otherwise constant mental stimuli. It's about giving your mind the space to wander and simply paying attention to what you're sensing without any particular agenda, purpose or self-criticism.

Mindfulness is relevant both when you are meditating and when you are not. Of course, a big part of meditation is allowing your mind to reconnect with the present in this way, and to loosen your grip on the worries and intrusive thoughts that threaten your peace. However, you can also work on being more mindful all the time - when you're working, interacting with others when you're going through a good time, or a more challenging time.

Mindfulness is both a key component to the practice of meditation as well as a way of life. Although, like meditation, its roots are in eastern philosophy, it bears similarities to the western ideology of stoicism.

This Ancient Greek school of thought pioneered by philosophers such as Seneca and Epictetus can still offer a fresh perspective on freeing ourselves from overthinking and living a more mindful life to this day. For instance, as put by Epictetus:

'When someone is properly grounded in life, they shouldn't have to look outside themselves for approval.'

Similarly, Seneca famously said:

'True happiness is to enjoy the present, without anxious dependence upon the future, not to amuse ourselves with either hopes or fears but to rest satisfied with what we have, which is sufficient, for he that is so, wants nothing.'

How To Meditate

Bearing all of this wisdom - ancient and modern; eastern and western - in mind, also note that the most successful way to meditate is to do so without too much expectation, and certainly without self-criticism. In truth, it doesn't actually matter how you're sitting, or whether or not you play music, or have the light on. You could do it lying down, in bed, in the bath, or at your desk. Whenever you get an opportunity to switch off for a few short moments, in order to give your mind that valuable reboot that it so craves, and continue your day with a newfound sense of mental clarity and purpose.

Don't fret if rogue thoughts enter your head, either. You haven't failed. Don't just throw in the towel or claim meditation to be stupid because you don't quite get it the first couple of attempts. The more you overthink about having a clear mind, or getting things done "how they are supposed to be," the more your rumination threatens your inner peace.

Simply allow your thought processes to flow organically, perhaps gently ushering them towards a key mantra or focus that you selected for your practice- for instance "I am exactly where I need to be," or "I will not worry about what I cannot control." Will all other chatter in the back of your mind to at least quieten into a soft hum. And then, just wait and see where your mind takes you once it is freed from its usual shackles of obsessive, compulsive thoughts.

Find your ideal meditation

Pranayama: Nadi Shodhana and Brahmari

I propose that the best meditation exercises, especially if you suffer from anxiety as a result of your overthinking, is 'Pranayama,' – which literally means 'control of breath.' I highly recommend, as a first step to using your physical body to calm your mind,

you start being more conscious of your breathing. At first, it may seem strange, but then you will realize that thinking about your breath is working diverting your thoughts from your worries.

The word "prana" alone means vital energy. According to ancient Hindu beliefs, this spiritual spark or energy source and the mind are intimately connected (and today, this is somewhat backed up from what scientists have discussed about the brain's electromagnetic waves!). In terms of this apparent duality between "prana" and the physical mind, the idea behind Pranayama meditation states that controlling one helps to balance out the other. However, when there is an imbalance between the two, both physical and mental complications can arise. Indeed, chronic overthinking is often a result of this imbalance between the mind and "prana." Bringing harmony between the "prana" and the mind is the aim of Pranayama meditation.

Pranayama Breathing Exercises for Overthinking

Okay, if all this talk of "prana" and spiritualism is a little far-fetched for your tastes, let's get to the science. Did you know that slowing down your breathing actually raises the carbon dioxide level in the blood? But this isn't as scary as it sounds. It is actually necessary for relaxation - for instance, while you are sleeping. This is because it tips its pH level back to a slightly more acidic and less alkaline state. As such,

the blood's pH decreases, and the nervous system naturally calms you down.

Your breath can be a hugely powerful ally when it comes to building the resilience to cope with temporary states of either mental, physical, or emotional strain—whether you're grappling with anger after being wronged by a loved one, having a stressful day at work, or are anxiously ruminating about a particular responsibility. A clearer mind will help any given situation - no matter how anxiety-ridden you may feel in the moment. Taking the time to control your breath can be truly life-changing.

It may feel strange and unnatural at first to be actively conscious of your own breathing. Breathing is an instinct, after all. We are born knowing how to do it. As such, it has become so habitual that it feels rather odd to give it much attention. However, although instinctual to breathe, the way in which you breathe is under your control – and is perhaps one of the most untapped tools when it comes to taking care of our bodies and minds.

You'll probably find that once you pay attention to your breathing, you are breathing much shallower and faster than would be best. Most of the time, we don't make use of the vast space in our lungs, and capacity for all that oxygenated air we are completely dependent on to survive. Considering oxygen is fundamental to our survival and is – for the most part – in abundant supply – we can be rather stingy with ourselves!

Breathe deeply. Let your chest become filled with the air at your disposal. Feel your body drink in the oxygen and let it dissipate throughout your system. You are alive. You have air to breathe. This is literally your number one priority. So allow yourself to just fill your mind with this thought alone – the same way you are filling your lungs.

Is that better?

There is so much more to meditative breathing exercises than that. Here are a few ancient Indian breathing exercises that you can try your hand at next time your overthinking is beginning to creep up again:

Nadi Shodhana Breathing

Nadi Shodhana breathing is intended to purify the mind and body while supplying the body with additional oxygen. This helps to sharpen concentration, and yet slows down thought-processes to a manageable level.

To give it a try, simply sit in an upright position. Form a fist in your right hand but leave the thumb, ring finger, and little finger sticking out. Then press the right thumb onto the right side of the nose to cut off the air supply from one nostril. Inhale deeply. Hold it. And finally, release the thumb and press the ring finger of that same hand onto the left nostril. Repeat the practice on this side, then continue alternating nostrils between three and ten times. You will finish feeling a lot calmer, and your mind a lot clearer.

Ujjayi Pranayama Breathing

Ujjayi Pranayama breathing, also known as the "ocean breath" practice, calms down the overthinking mind by soothing your nervous system. It has been proven to relieve insomnia and overthinking.

For this one, sit in an upright position again, this time lightly constricting the glottis (in your throat) so that you can hear a faint "snoring" sound as you breathe - this will help to slow it down. Inhale deeply through the nose, so that you are completely filling your lungs. Next, exhale completely, also through the nose. Repeat for as long as you need to - until your heart rate slows, calm begins to wash over you, and those obsessive or intrusive thoughts start to drift away with your breath.

Kapalbhati Breathing

Now for a slightly more advanced pranayama breathing exercise: Kapalbhati breathing is said to cleanse the mind, body, and spirit. Essentially, it works by sending more oxygen to the brain, allowing it to function more effectively, while also balancing the nervous system, and strengthening the digestive system.

You guessed it: start by sitting in an upright position; Rest your hands on your knees or lower abdomen and then inhale deeply through the nose. Next, contract your lower abdominal muscles, and release the breath in short bursts. After one minute has passed, most likely having completely emptied your lungs in around 65-70 short exhalation bursts, inhale deeply through the nose again, and then exhale slowly fully through the mouth. Then inhale deeply again and repeat these quick exhalations, gradually increasing the exhalation bursts per minute, if it feels comfortable to do so. Repeat only two or three times and see how you feel after.

Ajapa Japa Meditation

Ajapa Japa meditation is unique in its combination of meditation, pranayama breathing, and the final ingredient: mantra chanting. Mindfulness is also a big part of this one. "Ajapa Japa" literally translates as 'the awareness and experience of a mantra' in Sanskrit. You simply repeat a mantra of your choice. Make it something meaningful and personal to you – such as 'I will not worry about what I cannot change,' 'I am strong and can achieve whatever I want,' or 'everything I need is within me.'

Eventually, after many repeats, the mantra is said to "come to life" and forms part of your consciousness. By this stage, you no longer even need to actively repeat the mantra, because it has become so ingrained into your subconscious that you are now immersed in it – and hopefully, this seeps into your behaviors and thinking patterns! This level of meditation mastery can take anything from a few months, right up to several years, for the real pros. It may seem like a long game, but even when first starting this unique ancient practice, you start to feel the benefit. It should not be regarded as a chore, but a joy – a nourishing activity for your mind, and an opportunity for active, positive, self-talk that can actually shape how you see yourself and how you think through challenging situations. It is said to increase self-awareness, mental clarity, and encourage positive thinking and mindfulness.

But for this to work, you must practice detachment. Observe your thoughts, even the negative ones, but don't let them consume you. Don't wallow in the past or fear the future. Just allow yourself to be in the moment and focus on the one key message you would like to manifest through your mantra.

Brahmari Breathing

Brahmari breathing focuses on the tight-chested feeling that many anxious overthinkers are all-too-familiar with. This ancient practice is designed to calm the mind and open up the lungs at the same time, leaving your mind grounded, and your thoughts slowed. To practice Brahmari Pranayama, sit comfortably, with your spine straight, and your shoulders relaxed. Then close your eyes and take a few regular breaths - not forcing them to be neither deep or shallow, but just going with your natural rhythm. Then, take one deep breath through the nose to fill your lungs to full capacity. While you slowly exhale, make a humming sound. Hold this sound until you empty your lung cavity and need to inhale again. Then inhale through the nose again and repeat, humming through your exhalation. Continue by inhaling naturally and then exhaling with this sound for several minutes.

Practice this exercise for as long as you need to feel your optimum level of calm.

The longer you continue the hum, the more of a relaxing effect it is likely to have. However, note that pushing the limits of your natural lung capacity too far can only lead to even more stress. So don't force anything – this is supposed to be relaxing, not a strain!

How Meditation Helps Brain Function

Although much research has been done over the last few decades, the precise effects of meditation on our electroencephalographic (EEG) brain activity are still in the process of being defined.

There has been a huge surge in scientific studies on meditation in the last ten years. This piqued interest in such an ancient practice in the age of technology that allows for detailed brain imaging means that we can now approach meditation in a completely new light. These studies have demonstrated time and time again the various beneficial effects of meditative practices on one's perception, mental cognition, emotional processing, and even neuroplasticity (the ability for your brain to adapt and form new neural connections).

For instance, a recent analysis on neuroimaging studies over around 300 meditation practitioners revealed that practicing meditation is consistently associated with an adapted morphology of the prefrontal cortex and body awareness regions.

Although we are only just seeing the tip of the iceberg when it comes to the effect of meditation on the brain, due to the limitations of EEG imaging (this can only measure brain activity in real-time - and it's not easy to meditate in a cold doctor's office with probes attached to your head, being watched intently!) expert meditators have been shown to experience an increase in their Gamma waves, which suggests they are more able to reach an inner state of calm even when not meditating. These Gamma waves were initially dismissed as 'spare brain noise' when detected on the first EEG imaging tests - that's until it was discovered that these waves are highly active when the subject is in states of love, altruism, or so-called 'higher virtues'. So what could this mean? Whether or not you choose to read into it as evidence of spirituality or a higher power, one thing we can agree in is that a special type of brain activity can be reached only when we are filled with positivity, and literal "good vibes."

Gamma waves are also above the frequency of neuronal firing, so precisely how they are generated remains a mystery! They are the fastest, highest-frequency of brain waves and allow the simultaneous processing of information from different brain areas, passing information both rapidly and effortlessly. Could this relate to the flow state discussed earlier? When the brain is both in peak productivity and peak relaxation? The jury is still out when it comes to exactly what all of this means. But when it comes to how it affects your overthinking and meditation habit, just know that as the most "subtle" of the brainwave frequencies, the mind has to be at peace, to access them. As such, it's crucial to find the best time, emotionally balanced state, and the perfect frequency for successful, gamma-sparking meditation.

The Bottom Line: Fix your body, fix your mind

As we have now seen, mindfulness and meditation can be life-changing for those with over-active, over-analytical minds getting in the way of how they live their life. If up until now, you have been skeptical of meditation and its tangible benefits, or simply have tried and haven't had much luck in the past, with a little patience and an open mind, you can allow it to take you to a new realm of self-awareness and become an observer of your own thoughts in the true stoic sense.

Surely it speaks for itself that both eastern and western philosophies share this common threat of letting go of your thoughts, emotions, and distractions in order to find true peace and maintain mental clarity. Now that these ideologies are just entering the mainstream once again, as the pendulum is starting to swing back the other way after decades - or arguably, centuries - of consuming, performing, and thinking non-stop - the recent surge in popularity ma make it seem like a fad, but it is more of a renaissance! Is it any wonder, looking at how modern life has us more mentally stimulated, and yet emotionally disconnected than ever, that we are collectively craving a space to do and think nothing. Your body and mind are craving it, so listen!

Whether it's one of the breathing exercises detailed earlier, sitting still and allowing your thoughts to quieten, or simply striving to become more mindful and slow down in your day-to-day life - try to somehow slow down and reconnect with your mind. Give it the break and nourishment that it deserves.

Conclusions

To wrap up, let's go over the key messages that you can walk away with after putting down this book. What can you take away from this journey? How can you implement through the rest of your life, and become a little better at handling your thought patterns? How can you implement the techniques and messages you've learned into your own day-to-day life?

What have we learned about overthinking and anxiety?

I encourage you to take away the following key points on overthinking, armored with the knowledge you need to overcome this common habit, and become more present and fulfilled in your life.

First of all, although it may seem like you are the only one facing that tall unsurmountable wall of racing or intrusive thoughts when you start to spiral into an episode of rumination, rest assured that you are not alone. Almost everyone has faced a very similar inner turmoil at some point - many people go through it on the regular! But just as overthinking isn't a disorder or cause for major alarm, neither is it the best way for our minds to operate.

However, in order to achieve maximum productivity as well as maximum emotional wellbeing - we need a healthy, clear, and balanced state of mind.

Furthermore, you must focus on your present by forgiving the past, learning from mistakes, and practice self-forgiveness. Accept that you simply can't predict the future - as much as you may try! A better use of your time and mental energy would be to overcome your fear of failure and manage the pressure you put on yourself, thanks to social expectations.

As you will recall, a key part of being at peace with yourself is trusting your instincts. Of course, that doesn't mean believing that you are invincible, or that you can do no wrong. A degree of thinking and strategy is always required. But aim to let go of obsessive, niggling negativity that threatens to hold you back or deter you from reaching your goals, whatever they are. Or an irrational quest for perfection that means you will never feel ready or good enough - when you often already are!

To help you achieve this, you can try tapping into your flow state - that perfect balance between rest and stimulation in order to perform and feel your best whatever you do. Then, get rid of mental junk by practicing mental minimalism and decluttering your mind. Organize your mind at work by planning - but also including sufficient breaks within this plan. Recognize that taking breaks - just like eating, drinking and sleeping - are all a part of your success and mental clarity.

Just as you shouldn't overthink at work, don't overthink your relationships - and don't forget those telling studies I shared with you! The more you analyze your relationship, the more "problems" you will identify. We all have real problems, sure - but avoid thinking further problems into existence - that's the last thing any of us need!

Remember that you are not defined by your thoughts, but more so what you actually do. As such, it's key to change your habits. Incorporate an optimal daily routine for both your mental and physical health.

Change your environment when necessary. This means giving your mind a break by changing the scenery - whether that's working on something new for a while, taking a walk, or taking a shower! A quick and simple break from whatever it is that's setting your mind in a spin can be a humble yet transformative way to boost your brainpower while giving your mind a break from frantic overthinking.

Don't forget to strive for excellence instead of perfection. Try to be a "perfect imperfectionist" instead- by being productive but in a more healthy and balanced way, and stop chasing the unreachable and anxiety-fueling myth of perfection!

Fight chronic indecisiveness and decision fatigue by not sweating the small stuff and making room for the bigger issues in your life. You will now be able to implement the 40/70 rule of decision-making to avoid either diving in completely unprepared, or, on the opposite side of the spectrum, being too afraid to take any action unless you know every single detail - often meaning you either never take the action you need to, or only feel "prepared" when that ship has sailed....

You now also know the main causes of procrastination and why do you really put off the work you know you need to do - whether it's from a place of fear of failing, simply not giving yourself the mental energy required, or overthinking every detail to the point that you are too overwhelmed to begin... I hope you have now identified your own main obstacles, and how to get around these to stop procrastination from holding you back. Overall, you will recognize any self-sabotaging behaviors from now on: where they come from, and how to stop them in their tracks.

Finally, I am happy to have equipped you with the basic theories behind mindfulness and meditation, and how these ideologies can enable you to live more in the present, and feel both more self-motivated and calmer. You will now be pretty darn knowledgeable when it comes to how fixing your body is key to fixing your mind - as you cannot have one flourish without the other, as well as how to utilize the power of breathing and rest for mental clarity. Not to forget your now-thorough knowledge of the basics of pranayama breathing exercises - from your Nadi Shodhana to your Brahmari...

Okay, it may take some re-reading of that part for it all to sink in! But just think how cultured you will seem to bring up these terms at your next party... (You're very welcome!)

Stop Overthinking! Some Final Thoughts

It's true that we all naturally feel good when we have success, or feel validated by others. This drive to succeed, just as our tendency to think deeply, are not inherently unhealthy habits to keep. However, if you place too much of your worth or even identity down to this constantly just-out-of-reach idea of perfection, and dream of success that is always one more achievement away, we will never truly have inner-peace or calm the storm in your mind.

You must learn to feel fulfilled and worthy no matter what comes your way, and regardless of what you achieve. This is truly the most powerful way to lay your overthinking habit to rest - to simply be - and be content in doing so!

To understand that you are not perfect - because you are human. And to realize that making mistakes should not sentence you to a lifetime of ruminating over what went wrong, or berating yourself constantly in your mind, needlessly re-living any negative emotions you experienced...

Okay, I admit, it's easier said than done to break these habits of a lifetime that take root way back into childhood. That being said, you must start giving our own opinions the respect and consideration that they deserve, and learning to make peace both with your past and all the possible scenarios of the future, in order to focus on the present to live a fulfilled and mindful life.

So take a moment to reflect on what you truly want each day. No, not tomorrow - but right now. What do you need? The chances are, what you really need is a lot less than you think once you take away the worries of tomorrow. Imagine living most of your days in such a carefree manner, far away from any intrusive worries about what tomorrow may bring?

So next time your thoughts start to race, and you start to obsess about something irrationally, convincing yourself that the worst-case-scenario will happen, just remember where you're at right now: The oxygen entering your body; the absence of an immediate threat to your life. You are okay. And whatever is threatening your peace - most likely - can wait. Your own emotional wellbeing should not only take priority, but it is the key to your mental capacity anyway. Only when you are mentally sound can you have any hope of solving your problems anyway! So remember that next time your anxiety levels rise, and you lose all hope.

Your negative thoughts only matter as much as you let them. And although it sometimes doesn't feel like it, you have some level of control over your own peace of thoughts and the emotions that they inspire - and this control can be worked on with patience and practice. And once you open your eyes to your potential to manipulate what you let affect you mentally, you will experience true emotional resilience.

The Bottom Line

I initially promised you that if you manage to let go of damaging thoughts and mental habits, that your mind would feel lighter, clearer, and more resilient to tackle any real problems you have - with all the unnecessary worries no longer cluttering your precious mental space and draining your precious mental energy.

By now, I trust you have a deep understanding of what overthinking truly is - how it can be harmful and counterproductive – and perhaps most importantly, how you can overcome it and keep your mind a much clearer and healthier place to be. I trust you will now feel more driven, with a clearer direction in mind – both in terms of your success in life, but also in terms of how to improve your relationship with your own mind, and how to reconnect with yourself to stop being a slave to your anxiety, unconscious worries and intrusive thoughts.

To finish with a quote by the 14th century Persian Poet, Hafez, that I hope will allow you to walk away today with the right mindset:

"Now that your worry has proved such an unlucrative business, Why not find a better job?"

Sebastian O'Brien

References

4 Reasons to Stop Worrying About the Future. (2012, July 26). Retrieved May 20, 2020, from https://www.embracethechaos.com/2012/07/4-reasons-to-stop-worrying-about-the-future/

6 Tips for Overcoming Anxiety-Related Procrastination. (2013). Retrieved June 10, 2020, from https://www.psychologytoday.com/us/blog/in-practice/201303/6-tips-overcoming-anxiety-related-procrastination

8 Ways to Stop Self-Sabotaging Your Success. (2018). Retrieved June 10, 2020, from https://www.entrepreneur.com/article/324900

Aldrey, M. (2019, June 8). Leverage Your Unique Energy Levels for Maximum Productivity. Retrieved May 21, 2020, from https://groovywink.com/energy-maximum-productivity/

Assari, S. (2016, June 22). Why stress is more likely to cause depression in men than in women. Retrieved from https://theconversation.com/why-stress-is-more-likely-to-cause-depression-in-men-than-in-women-57624

Azimy, R. (2020a, January 10). Somatic Experiencing: Restoring Balance to Heal Trauma. Retrieved from https://www.selfishdarling.com/2019/12/28/somatic-experiencing-restoring-balance-to-heal-trauma/

Azimy, R. (2020b, January 11). Alternatives to meditation for chatty minds. Retrieved June 17, 2020, from https://www.selfishdarling.com/inspiration/alternatives-to-meditation-for-chatty-minds/

Azimy, R. (2020c, April 3). The Secret to Contentment? Treat Your Emotions like the Weather. Retrieved May 18, 2020, from https://medium.com/illumination/the-secret-to-contentment-treat-yor-emotions-like-the-weather-bc7a51fc9e1a

Azimy, R. (2020d, April 27). So You Want to be More "ZEN"? - ILLUMINATION. Retrieved June 17, 2020, from https://medium.com/illumination/so-you-want-to-be-more-zen-65def826ab09?source=---------16------------------

Azimy, R. (2020e, May 4). Deepak Chopra's Meditation Challenge: 6 Lessons I Learned. Retrieved May 18, 2020, from https://www.selfishdarling.com/holistic-healing/deepak-chopras-meditation-challenge-6-lessons-i-learned/

Baer, D. (2015, April 28). The scientific reason why Barack Obama and Mark Zuckerberg wear the same outfit every day. Retrieved June 4, 2020, from https://www.businessinsider.com/barack-obama-mark-zuckerberg-wear-the-same-outfit-2015-4?r=US&IR=T

Boogaard, K. (2020, May 11). The Little-Known Reason You're So Indecisive. Retrieved June 4, 2020, from https://www.themuse.com/advice/the-littleknown-reason-youre-so-indecisive

Boyes, A. (2018, May 16). How to Stop Sabotaging Yourself. Retrieved June 10, 2020, from https://greatergood.berkeley.edu/article/item/how_to_stop_sabotaging_yourself

Cameron, K. S., & Spreitzer, G. M. (2012). *The Oxford Handbook of Positive Organizational Scholarship*. Oxford, United Kingdom: Oxford University Press.

Cannon, J. (2016, July 13). We All Want to Fit In. Retrieved May 27, 2020, from https://www.psychologytoday.com/us/blog/brainstorm/201607/we-all-want-fit-in

D. (2020a, January 6). 4 Types of Procrastination and How to Beat Them. Retrieved June 10, 2020, from https://alphaefficiency.com/4-types-procrastination-beat/

Daskal, L. (2020a, February 6). 10 Simple Ways You Can Stop Yourself From Overthinking. Retrieved May 20, 2020, from https://www.inc.com/lolly-daskal/10-simple-ways-you-can-stop-yourself-from-overthinking.html

Daskal, L. (2020b, February 6). 10 Simple Ways You Can Stop Yourself From Overthinking. Retrieved July 1, 2020, from https://www.inc.com/lolly-daskal/10-simple-ways-you-can-stop-yourself-from-overthinking.html

Day, S. (n.d.). Stress Nutrition Advice - Nutritionist Resource. Retrieved June 11, 2020, from https://www.nutritionist-resource.org.uk/articles/stress.html#stressanddiet

Dean, C. (2019, July 1). What Is Mental Minimalism. Retrieved May 20, 2020, from https://www.clarissadean.com/blog/mental-minimalism

deloitteeditor. (2017, May 12). How Stress Affects Team Dynamics. Retrieved May 14, 2020, from https://deloitte.wsj.com/cmo/2017/01/19/how-stress-affects-team-dynamics/

Developing a Mental Framework for Effective Thinking. (2020, January 3). Retrieved May 20, 2020, from https://fs.blog/2015/03/mental-framework/

Dollard, Maureen F, Dormann, C., Tuckey, M. R., & Escartín, J. (2017). Psychosocial safety climate (PSC) and enacted PSC for workplace bullying and psychological health problem reduction. *European Journal of Work and Organizational Psychology*, 26(6), 844–857. https://doi.org/10.1080/1359432x.2017.1380626

Dollard, M.F., Dormann, C., & Idris, A. M. (2019). *Psychosocial Safety Climate: A New Work Stress Theory* (1st ed. 2019 ed.). Heidelberg, Denmark: Springer.

Dunne, C. (2019, June 6). The Power of Single-Tasking. Retrieved May 21, 2020, from https://www.tameday.com/the-power-of-single-tasking/

Edberg, H. (2020, May 14). How to Stop Overthinking Everything: 12 Simple Habits. Retrieved June 18, 2020, from https://www.positivityblog.com/how-to-stop-overthinking/

Editor, HRreview. (2019, August 9). It costs over £30K to replace a staff member. Retrieved May 19, 2020, from https://www.hrreview.co.uk/hr-news/recruitment/it-costs-over-30k-to-replace-a-staff-member/50677

Everything You NEED to Know About The 40/70 Rule! (n.d.). Retrieved June 4, 2020, from https://marketingreleased.com/everything-you-need-to-know-about-the-4070-rule/

Fader, S. (2017, June 2). What Is Overthinking Disorder? | BetterHelp. Retrieved from https://www.betterhelp.com/advice/personality-disorders/what-is-overthinking-disorder/

Fahkry, T. (2018, June 20). Here's Why You Are Not Your Thoughts. Retrieved May 21, 2020, from https://medium.com/the-mission/heres-why-you-are-not-your-thoughts-5459b0b96ba0

Fields, K. (2017, May 15). The Imperfection of Perfectionism. Retrieved May 27, 2020, from https://www.talkspace.com/blog/the-imperfection-of-perfectionism/

Fletcher, B. (2019, June 20). Struggling to sleep? How to avoid overthinking when you get in to bed. Retrieved May 21, 2020, from https://www.netdoctor.co.uk/healthy-living/a28687/overthinking-cant-sleep/

How Perfectionism Can Contribute to Anxiety. (2020, March 22). Retrieved May 27, 2020, from https://www.verywellmind.com/perfectionism-and-panic-disorder-2584391#

How to Cure the Perfectionist Habit. (2013, December 2). Retrieved May 27, 2020, from https://gatorworks.net/how-to-cure-the-perfectionist-habit/

How to support mental health at work. (2020, April 30). Retrieved May 26, 2020, from https://www.mentalhealth.org.uk/publications/how-support-mental-health-work

Huffington, A. (2014a). *Thrive*. Zaltbommel, Netherlands: Van Haren Publishing.

Huffington, A. (2014b). *Thrive*. Zaltbommel, Netherlands: Van Haren Publishing.

Increased Gamma Brainwave Amplitude Compared to Control in Three Different Meditation Traditions. (2017, January 24). Retrieved June 17, 2020, from https://www.ncbi.nlm.nih.gov/pmc/articles/PMC5261734/

Insights Discovery part 1: The 4 colors. (2018). Retrieved June 12, 2020, from https://www.mudamasters.com/en/personal-growth-personality/insights-discovery-part-1-4-colors

Jones, M. (2018, September 11). 5 Ways Minimalism Is Good For Your Mental Health. Retrieved May 20, 2020, from https://www.aconsciousrethink.com/6881/minimalism-mental-health/

Jordan, R. (2019, July 26). How to Stop Overthinking. Retrieved June 17, 2020, from https://www.yogi.press/home/how-to-stop-overthinking

Kahn, W. A. (1990). Psychological Conditions of Personal Engagement and Disengagement at Work. *Academy of Management Journal, 33*(4), 692–724. https://doi.org/10.5465/256287

Kumar, M. (2009, December 7). Difference Between Reflection and Introspection. Retrieved from http://www.differencebetween.net/miscellaneous/difference-between-reflection-and-introspection/

Markway, B. (2013, January 14). Pursuing Excellence, Not Perfection. Retrieved May 26, 2020, from https://www.psychologytoday.com/us/blog/shyness-is-nice/201301/pursuing-excellence-not-perfection+

Maros, M. (2016, October 31). How to Deal with Indecision. Retrieved June 4, 2020, from https://peacefulmindpeacefullife.org/how-to-deal-with-indecision/

Morin, A. (2019a, January 19). 10 Signs You're an Overthinker. Retrieved June 22, 2020, from https://thriveglobal.com/stories/signs-you-overthink-things/

Morin, A. (2019b, October 15). The Difference Between Helpful Problem Solving And Harmful Overthinking. Retrieved from https://www.forbes.com/sites/amymorin/2019/10/15/the-difference-between-helpful-problem-solving-and-harmful-overthinking/#3dc86c156e5f

Nwatarali, G. (2018, May 5). 5 Tips To Overcome Laziness And Procrastination. Retrieved June 10, 2020, from https://lifestylebusinessmag.com/5-tips-overcome-laziness-procrastination/

Oracles, T. (2019, June 25). 11 Genius Tips to Be More Decisive. Retrieved June 4, 2020, from https://www.success.com/11-genius-tips-to-be-more-decisive/

Oshin, M. (2019, May 23). Elon Musks' "3-Step" First Principles Thinking: How to Think and Solve Difficult Problems Like a.... Retrieved May 20, 2020, from https://medium.com/the-mission/elon-musks-3-step-first-principles-thinking-how-to-think-and-solve-difficult-problems-like-a-ba1e73a9f6c0

Perfection and Anxiety:How Perfection Can Increase Anxiety. (n.d.). Retrieved May 26, 2020, from https://discoverymood.com/blog/perfectionism-can-increase-anxiety/

Peterson, C., & Seligman, M. (2004). *Character Strengths and Virtues: A Handbook and Classification* (1st ed.). Oxford, United Kingdom: American Psychological Association / Oxford University Press.

Peterson, Christopher, & Park, N. (2006). Character strengths in organizations. *Journal of Organizational Behavior, 27*(8), 1149–1154. https://doi.org/10.1002/job.398

Petticrew, M. P., Lee, K., & McKee, M. (2012). Type A Behavior Pattern and Coronary Heart Disease: Philip Morris's "Crown Jewel." *American Journal of Public Health, 102*(11), 2018–2025. https://doi.org/10.2105/ajph.2012.300816

Pfeffer, J. (2018, May 3). How your workplace is killing you. Retrieved June 19, 2020, from https://www.bbc.com/worklife/article/20180502-how-your-workplace-is-killing-you

Porath, C., Spreitzer, G., Gibson, C., & Garnett, F. G. (2011). Thriving at work: Toward its measurement, construct validation, and theoretical refinement. *Journal of Organizational Behavior, 33*(2), 250–275. https://doi.org/10.1002/job.756

Qureshi, H. (2018, January 29). Being in the zone: A matter of extreme focus. Retrieved May 20, 2020, from https://medium.com/@HassanQureshi/being-in-the-zone-a-matter-of-extreme-focus-7d37585c75b4

Raman, R. (2018, June 21). 11 Simple Ways To Stop Overthinking Everything And Take Control Of Your Life. Retrieved May 21, 2020, from https://medium.com/the-mission/11-simple-ways-to-stop-overthinking-everything-and-take-control-of-your-life-cf6de0b8d83f

Ravi Raman. (2018, February 22). Meditation is the Ultimate Life Hack You Aren't Using. Retrieved June 17, 2020, from https://raviraman.com/meditation-life-hack/

Rosen, R. (2007, August 28). Pranayama Practices for Stress, Anxiety, and Depression. Retrieved June 17, 2020, from https://www.yogajournal.com/yoga-101/inhale-exhale-relax-and-energize

Ruggeri, A. (2018). The dangerous downsides of perfectionism. Retrieved May 26, 2020, from https://www.bbc.com/future/article/20180219-toxic-perfectionism-is-on-the-rise

Self-Sabotage: Overcoming Self-Defeating Behavior. (n.d.). Retrieved June 10, 2020, from https://www.mindtools.com/pages/article/newTCS_95.htm

Sinicki, A. (2017, January 7). The Philosophy of Bruce Lee - On Flow, Self-Actualization, Creativity, Willpower and More. Retrieved May 20, 2020, from https://www.thebioneer.com/philosophy-bruce-lee-flow-self-actualization-creativity-willpower/

Stress Puts Double Whammy On Reproductive System, Fertility. (2009). Retrieved May 14, 2020, from https://www.sciencedaily.com/releases/2009/06/090615171618.htm

Symptoms That Mimic Epilepsy LInked to Stress, Poor Coping Skills - 04/10/2012. (2012). Retrieved May 18, 2020, from https://www.hopkinsmedicine.org/news/media/releases/symptoms_that_mimic_epilepsy_linked_to_stress_poor_coping_skills

Systolic Blood Pressure Intervention Trial (SPRINT) Study | National Heart, Lung, and Blood Institute (NHLBI). (2018, July 25). Retrieved June 12, 2020, from https://www.nhlbi.nih.gov/science/systolic-blood-pressure-intervention-trial-sprint-study

Teeth grinding (bruxism). (2020, May 11). Retrieved May 25, 2020, from https://www.nhs.uk/conditions/teeth-grinding/

The future of future-oriented cognition in non-humans: theory and the empirical case of the great apes. (2014, November 5). Retrieved May 18, 2020, from https://www.ncbi.nlm.nih.gov/pmc/articles/PMC4186238/

the Healthline Editorial Team. (2017, September 28). 5 Steps for Overcoming Indecision. Retrieved June 4, 2020, from https://www.healthline.com/health/5-steps-overcoming-indecision

Thibodeaux, W. (2020, February 6). The 3 Main Types of Procrastinators, According to Psychology. Retrieved June 10, 2020, from https://www.inc.com/wanda-thibodeaux/the-3-main-types-of-procrastinators-according-to-psychology.html

Trapani, G. (2012, August 4). Work Smart: Do Your Worst Task First (Or, Eat a Live Frog Every Morning). Retrieved May 21, 2020, from https://www.fastcompany.com/1592454/work-smart-do-your-worst-task-first-or-eat-live-frog-every-morning

(1970, January 19). How To Stop Overthinking Everything, According To Therapists. Retrieved from https://www.buzzfeed.com/ryanhowes/how-to-stop-ruminating

Weiss, S. (2017, December 11). 7 Reasons Why You're So Indecisive, According To Experts. Retrieved June 4, 2020, from https://www.bustle.com/p/7-reasons-why-youre-so-indecisive-according-to-experts-7427785

Y. (2019, November 28). The Different Types of Pranayama and When to Use Them. Retrieved June 17, 2020, from https://www.yogamatters.com/blog/different-types-of-pranayama-when-to-use-them/

Yeong, D. (2020). Why Tiny Actions Work Best, Way Better than Massive Action. Retrieved May 21, 2020, from https://deanyeong.com/tiny-actions-work-best/

Z. (2020b, May 11). Finding Flow: 5 Steps to Get in the Zone and Be More Productive. Retrieved May 20, 2020, from https://zapier.com/blog/how-to-find-flow/

Zimmer, C. (2007, April 2). Time in the Animal Mind. Retrieved May 18, 2020, from https://www.nytimes.com/2007/04/03/science/03time.html

Printed in Great Britain
by Amazon